Introduction

The Legacy of Totoliguoqui

In 1913, a Mayo Indian[1] called Miguel Totoliguoqui (almost certainly a nom de guerre, meaning "cock's foot" in Mayo) amassed a small army of Mayos at the top of the Cerro del Bayájorit, the sole peak in the broad expanse of the Mayo valley's alluvial plain. From this stronghold, the Indians, armed with bows and arrows and a few firearms, proceeded to attack the recently established haciendas of the Mestizo overlords in the most fertile regions of the valley. According to oral reports, the goal apparently was to eradicate the still-small minority of non-Mayos in the valley, which until 1889 had been under the autonomous control of the Mayos.

Although the Mestizos, representatives of the national culture and polity of Mexico, were a numerical minority at the time of Totoliguoqui's uprising, the force of the national authorities was on their side; they also had more guns. The result of this unequal confrontation was that Totoliguoqui and his lieutenants were captured and summarily executed by the Mexican army at El Citavaro, near the village of Júpare.

Although the story of Totoliguoqui may seem to be merely one of hundreds of accounts of pathetic attempts by Native Americans to withstand the onslaught of the bearers of European culture, for the present-day residents of the Mayo valley it remains a watershed event in the history of the region. Totoliguoqui's defeat was the last chapter in a long history of Spanish and Mexican attempts to subdue the Mayos--attempts that, more than

---

1. The term "Indian" was imposed upon the natives of the New World by the first Spanish explorers, who believed that they had discovered India. In this way, the extremely diverse cultures of this vast region were lumped together into one inaccurate category. Nevertheless, the term is used today in common parlance as well as in the anthropological literature. Keeping in mind that the Mayo culture is distinct from other Native American cultures, the word Indian will be used to refer to them in this text.

almost any others in the history of North America, had met with failure after failure. Thus, the final success of the Mestizos is significant to this day for the inhabitants of the valley. In many ways, they are all descendants of Totoliguoqui.

The Mayo valley is at the southernmost edge of the present-day state of Sonora, Mexico (see Figure 1). Because of its great distance from the capital, in addition to frequent Indian insurrections on the northern and southern borders of the state, Sonora was for the most part ignored by Spanish and later Mexican officials until the late 19th century (Hu-DeHart 1984:12; Acuña 1974:2). The region was officially incorporated into the Spanish empire in the 16th century and later established as a separate province with its own capital. The number of Spanish and Mestizo settlers was quite small, however, and they were clustered in the mining regions of the mountains and the northern river valleys, whose indigenous populations were sparse or had been eliminated by conquest and disease. The large, fertile valleys of the Yaqui and Mayo rivers in the southern part of Sonora had been left alone not only by Spanish and Mexican government officials but by the settlers themselves; and from the time of the expulsion of the Jesuits from Spanish territory in 1767, the Yaqui and Mayo residents of these valleys retained economic and political autonomy. This situation was by no means the result of benign neglect on the part of the would-be settlers; rather, the legendary military efficacy of the Indians against all attempts to take over their territory maintained their power.

It was not until Porfirio Díaz became President of Mexico in 1877 that Sonora began to play a significant part in the political and economic affairs of the nation. Díaz' policies initiated the successful encroachment on both Mayo and Yaqui lands. It was this encroachment, and the virtual enslavement of the Mayo population under the brutal hacienda system almost unknown in the region prior to Díaz, that Totoliguoqui and his followers sought to reverse.

The 1910 Revolution ousted Díaz, but its effects had not yet been felt in the Mayo valley by 1913. On the contrary, the Mestizos who had been encouraged by Díaz to pursue their agricultural enterprises continued this process in the aftermath of the Totoliguoqui uprising. No longer wary of Mayo resistance, Mestizos expanded irrigation and road systems and encroached further on Mayo land. Thus the defeat of Totoliguoqui spelled an end to Mayo hopes for autonomy and opened the floodgates for the Mestizo influx that has characterized most of this century's history in the valley.

The immediate effect of the events of 1913 was the increased power of Mestizo landowners in the valley. The long-term ramifications of Totoliguoqui's defeat pervade most aspects of the history of the region and of contemporary life there. For example, the Mayos decided to participate in the military campaign of Alvaro Obregón, which had begun in 1912, because they saw the Revolution not only as a way of regaining ground lost under Díaz, but also to make up for Totoliguoqui's defeat. Their participation was

Introduction

instrumental in bringing Obregón to power and in assuring their own final betrayal. The bitterness still felt by Mayos today as a result of this betrayal is one legacy of Totoliguoqui's defeat.

The betrayal of the Mayos stems from the agricultural development project instituted by the postrevolutionary government. The massive irrigation district and the extensive technical innovations introduced in the area, combined with official favoring of large landholdings, disenfranchised the majority of contemporary descendants of the original Mayo inhabitants. Those who gained the most from the development project were wealthy Mestizo landowners who gained title to former Mayo lands. The result is a situation of extremes in wealth and poverty. Today, people who speak Mayo and adhere to Mayo folk-religious beliefs form a small minority of the valley's residents; they are also its poorest. These are the cultural descendants of Totoliguoqui.

However, in a broader sense all the residents of the valley are his descendants, for all share in some way the legacy of his defeat. Before 1889, interaction between Mayos and Mestizos was that of two distinct political, economic and social entities. The defeat of Totoliguoqui confirmed militarily what the treaty of 1889 had put into writing: the Mayos were now a subjugated ethnic minority within the Mexican political and economic system. The ethnic boundary has blurred considerably in the years since 1913, and many genetic descendants of Mayos no longer adhere to Mayo culture. However, there exists in some communities an ongoing undercurrent of ethnic conflict despite economic and ethnic change. Other communities continue to have pride in their Mayo heritage, despite the onus of Mayo identity in the region as a whole. Both of these patterns derive from the legacy of Totoliguoqui. As for the genetic descendants of the Mestizos, they too share in this legacy, for it was the events of 1913 that made it possible for the Mestizos to become the dominant ethnic and economic segment in the valley. The story of the Mayos' struggle, and the process that created the economic and ethnic situation of today, is told in Chapter One.

Why the Mayo Valley?

My interest in the Mayo valley stems from my more general interest in ethnic minorities and the relationship between economic change and ethnic identity.[2] Although these broad topics could conceivably be investigated almost anywhere in Latin America, the Mayo region is particularly suited for several reasons. Perhaps the most compelling of these is the mammoth agricultural development project constructed by the national government in the 1950s; this project brought about some of the most rapid economic

---

2. The original field work for this study was funded by the Doherty Foundation and by National Science Foundation Grant #BNS-77-18081.

growth ever documented. The question of how the Mayos, now an ethnic minority, were affected by this change is an intriguing one. Also, there is a certain amount of controversy in the anthropological literature concerning how and to what extent the economic change in the valley has affected the ethnicity of its inhabitants. Charles Erasmus (1961) documented the overall effects of the change and predicted that Mayo identity would ultimately disappear because of the economic opportunities available in the valley. The subtitle of N. Ross Crumrine's 1977 book, "A People Who Refuse to Die," brought this prediction into question. This controversy provided the backdrop for my own research.

Given the nature of existing works on ethnic identity, I arrived in the Mayo valley expecting to find two distinct groups, Mayos and Mestizos. Further, I expected to find that Mayos were changing into Mestizos. My goal was to discover more precisely how and why this process was occurring and in which kinds of communities. Accordingly, I set about interviewing key informants and carrying out participant observation in the communities I had selected. To my surprise, I found that no two informants could provide an identical or in some cases even a similar set of criteria for distinguishing the two ethnic categories. On the other hand, everyone could identify to which group their own and other families in the community belonged. Finally, no one seemed able or willing to identify individuals who had changed ethnic identity.

This perplexing set of circumstances caused me a great deal of frustration during the first few months of field work. My thoughts on these matters were influenced by one informant's answer to my question as to his ethnicity. He replied, "Más *yoreme* que *de razón*," more Mayo than Mestizo, thereby implying a continuum between the two. Enlightened by the new perspective provided by this view, I began seeing evidence of a cultural continuum in many different contexts. My informants, elated that I had finally understood the situation, were happy to point out where different individuals and families were on this continuum, while still maintaining that all were either Mayo or Mestizo. I also began to discern the situations which especially elicited Mayo or Mestizo behavior. The details of these discoveries, as well as the process of permanent ethnic change, form much of the text of this monograph. The theoretical bases for these processes are discussed more fully in Chapter Two.

The Mayo folk-Catholic fiesta system, one aspect of village life that I had thought relatively unimportant in my original theoretical formulations, turned out to be central to an understanding of ethnicity in the region. Active participation in the elaborate cycle of religious and social rituals is one certain criterion for Mayo identity. At the same time, the fiesta for each village's patron saint is the most important ritual and social event of the year for everyone in the community. As such, it provides a central forum for situational ethnicity and in some cases for demonstrating a family's change along the cultural continuum. Because of the importance of the fiesta system,

Introduction

and the complexity of the system itself, Chapter Three is devoted to a detailed description of the fiesta cycle and how it fits into the overall ethnic landscape.

My original framework was comparative: I expected to find that different kinds of communities would have different kinds of economic and social opportunities, and that these opportunities would determine the extent of ethnic change. Because the region is predominantly agricultural, I chose access to land as the basis for differentiating communities. There are essentially three types of landholding in the region: *ejido*, private and *comunidad indígena*. Ejidos are land-grant communities organized by the government. Each family has access to a plot of land, but the land cannot be rented or sold. Private land is for the most part held in immense plots owned by the wealthy, who have benefited most from the economic development program. The few small private plots are minuscule, ranging from one to three hectares[3]; there is no middle range of private plot size. Comunidades indígenas are similar to U.S. Indian reservations. In the Mayo region, the comunidades hold their land communally, primarily because they are outside the irrigation district and cannot farm owing to the natural aridity of the region. A more detailed discussion of these ecological, economic, and political entities is found in Chapter Four.

The communities I worked in consisted of two villages in the irrigation district and three hamlets in the Masiaca comunidad indígena. I chose the villages because they are of similar population size but otherwise different. Júpare has a substantial number of private landowners, and both the private and ejido plots are quite small, while Buaysiacobe is made up entirely of ejido families whose plots are comparatively large. The comunidad hamlets, because they have no access to irrigation water, are obviously the poorest of the communities in the study. Another criterion affected my choice of communities: all had been studied previously by either Crumrine or Erasmus.

Although many of my original reasons for choosing these communities turned out to be relatively unimportant, the differences among them do affect in many ways the processes of ethnic change and situational ethnicity in each. The reasons for the differences in this process are described in greater detail in Chapters Five, Six and Seven.

The Anthropologist as Female

The day before I left for the Mayo region, one of the professors in my department told me that he thought I had an interesting project, but that I would not be able to carry it out because none of the men would talk to me. Surprised and somewhat alarmed at this news, I asked him why the men

---

3. A hectare measures 2.5 acres.

would not talk to me. He said it was because I was a woman, and men in this region will not talk to women. This possibility had not occurred to me, possibly because I had always assumed that my gender was not an important factor in my professional life. I decided to continue in this assumption until proven wrong by events.

When I arrived in the Mayo region, I discovered that being a woman did have certain impacts on my work, although fortunately not those predicted by the professor. The role of women in rural Mexican society is quite different from that of women in urban United States settings, and many, if not most, of my activities were incompatible with that role. For example, women in rural Mexico do not live alone or travel alone. Married women do not leave their husbands to live in a foreign country for 13 months. Women do not approach strange men and engage them in conversations about their personal lives.

By living with a family, I complied with one of these rules at least; however, I broke all the other conventions listed above and almost certainly many others. At first, no one believed I was married, because if I were I would not have been able to get permission from my husband to leave my home. When told I had not asked his permission, everyone became certain I could not be married. When asked if I carried a gun in the glove compartment of my car for protection when traveling alone, I said "no" and again amazed my informants. By approaching men whom I knew to be community leaders and speaking to them, I became the object of widespread astonishment.

All of this breaking of accepted rules certainly might have backfired, and I worried not a little that my behavior might indeed lead to a situation where neither the men nor the women would talk to me. For a few months, it is true, I had trouble persuading people to tell me more than the barest details of their lives and the events in their communities. I never believed that my being a woman was the reason for this difficulty, however, and there did come a time when informants--male and female--became friends who told me sometimes more than I wanted to hear about themselves, their families, their neighbors, and their neighbors' families, ad infinitum.

The question of my marital status, and all that it entailed in defining my role, was resolved by a visit from my husband a few months after I began my field work. The proof that I really was married, and that my husband "gave me permission" to work not only away from our home but so very far away, placed me in a unique category and made me so unusual that most of my informants stopped expecting my behavior to conform to any accepted female roles. Over time, my initially controversial behavior became the subject of comment and questioning from informants rather than shock and consternation.

As for protecting myself while traveling alone, I really never felt the need. Although the homicide rate is high throughout rural Mexico, there is nothing that could be described as banditry or random sexual violence in

Introduction

Sonora. Indeed, barring the possibility of becoming lost in the uncharted maze of dirt tracks that make up much of the Mayo valley, I believe I was never in any great danger. Even getting lost was not really a problem, for there was always the certainty that there would be a hamlet nearby where I could get information.

In the context of the overall pandemonium of the large annual fiestas, again I felt in no danger, despite dire warnings from Mestizo townspeople. Consumption of large amounts of alcohol by all men at the fiestas is de rigueur, and results in a certain amount of aggressive behavior on their part. Although I was at first apprehensive about being the only female observer of certain parts of the fiestas--notably the ritual dancing--I felt it a necessary part of my research, and found that I was not discouraged from observing. My only vaguely negative experience in this context was the not infrequent desire by one or two of the more inebriated men to "explain" to me what was going on. Other onlookers would allow such an individual to go far enough to be entertaining, but on no occasion did I feel threatened. There was always a general consensus, albeit unspoken, that I would be protected from random violence by the clearer heads present in any potentially volatile situation.

Whenever I am asked if I have difficulty doing field work in Mexico *as a woman*, my reply is always that doing field work anywhere is difficult for everyone. Living in a situation where no one else has any idea what one is doing; where one has no privacy and is working during every waking moment; where one is asking difficult questions and often receiving perplexing answers--these universal difficulties far outweigh any that I may have had simply because I am female.

It is perhaps best not to place too great an importance on the role of gender in field research. Had I tried, for example, to conform more to the role of women in rural Mexico, it is possible that I might have had more difficulty: in order to get the information I needed for my research, I had to behave in a way contrary to that role. By being completely outside the conventional role, I became, ultimately, an accepted anomaly whose own patterns of behavior were the subject of inquiry from my informants. It may be argued, of course, that I lost certain kinds of data that are available only to men because there are certain topics men will not discuss even with anomalous women. At the same time, however, I was privy to conversations on subjects only discussed by women. Most important, I firmly believe that the central topics of my research were impersonal enough and unrelated enough to gender that the data I collected are as reliable as those collected by the men before me. Were it otherwise, I would not have written this monograph.

Field Methods

There has been some discussion in social science journals concerning what is the "best" field method. Some assert that participant observation yields the most complete data (Becker and Geer 1957), while others contend that it does not provide a broad enough base of information (Babchuk 1962). It has also been noticed that different kinds of methods lead to different interpretations of similar phenomena (Walton 1966). This last finding suggests that perhaps the "best" method is a combination of participant observation, informal interviewing and structured questionnaires.

It is easy to take this stand in theory; few would doubt its validity. In practice, it has logical contradictions. For example, the participant observer tries to become a part of the society observed; this role is somewhat incongruous with that of the interviewer asking structured questions. Although there is a certain amount of tension between the methods, however, they are not necessarily mutually exclusive.

My own field methods included participant observation, open-ended interviews, and structured interviews which nevertheless became somewhat open-ended in that interviewees sometimes gave answers I had not anticipated. Although I never completely overcame the incongruity of these three methods, I succeeded to some extent by using only one method at a time. For example, at ejido meetings and fiestas I was only a participant observer and never tried to interview individuals beyond asking the meaning of certain behaviors. Similarly, when conducting structured interviews I kept to the interviews, except when etiquette required more informal behavior.

I believe this combination to be an effective one, for it yields different kinds of information that check each other. Structured interviews elicit statistical information that confirms or denies the intuitive and impressionistic data produced by participant observation. However, without participant observation and open-ended interviews it would be difficult to know what questions to ask in questionnaires, or how to interpret the answers.

In order to gain some basic knowledge of each community, and to establish ties with community leaders, my first method was to tape interviews with both secular and religious leaders. Because of the difficulty in making personal contacts with individual families at first, my methods were confined to these interviews and participant observation at public events for the first two months of the study. During this time, I also began my study of the Mayo language with a man who became one of my key informants, as well as a good friend, over the course of the project.

The formality of my role at public events during the first two months makes it inaccurate to describe my method as anything but nonparticipant observation. I was seen as an honored guest, but my presence was not well understood and my relationship with those present was purely formal. Over

Introduction

time, I became a known figure at these events and gradually became accepted in public contexts.

In the meantime, I used past unstructured interviews as pretexts to make informal visits to the interviewees, trying to get some idea of daily life and its variety. Although my presence was ignored or joked about at these informal gatherings, my halting and sometimes hilarious efforts to learn and practice Mayo gradually ingratiated me, and eventually I became an expected visitor. It is true, however, that my in-depth knowledge of daily life derives from a close relationship with only a few families in each community. This is the nature of participant observation, but its limitation on breadth is made up for by the intensive kind of knowledge that it provides.

Without the kind of rapport that is established only by participant observation, it would probably have been impossible to ask and receive answers to the questions in the structured interviews. Because I had become a known entity, I was able to conduct my "census," as it was called, without arousing the fear and suspicion that surrounds any stranger who is asking questions and writing down the answers.

There were two kinds of structured interviews in the study. The first consisted of extensive interviews with major participants in the Mayo religious system. It is clear both from the literature and from my participant observation that an understanding of this system and of who participates in it are keys to comprehending ethnic identity in the region. The second type of structured interview was broader, based on a 15% household sample in each community. The nature of this sample demonstrates the difficulty of applying statistical methods to rural peasant communities. The lack of census data on these communities in particular made dependence on informants greater than would be the case in the United States. However, raw data supplied by the Instituto Nacional Indigenista (INI) and the Comité Nacional para la Eradicación del Paludismo (CNEP) were very useful in suggesting the approximate ethnic composition of the communities and the number of households in each.

Analysis of Data

The analysis of data from participant observation and key informant interviews was an ongoing process throughout my field work and after I left the research area. An example of how this method works can be seen in the way that I came to understand ethnicity in the various communities. During the first several months of field work, I was constantly perplexed at the ways that people responded to my questions concerning ethnic identity. These questions became the source of much entertainment for my informants. I slowly came to the realization that, rather than two distinct ethnic categories, there was a continuum of cultural traits and symbols which was manipulated according to situation. This realization came as a result of constant rereading of field notes and rechecking of information from informants. When I presented the concept of the cultural continuum, using as an analogy a line in the dirt with dots showing the different families, I was greeted with nods and smiles--I had finally understood what everyone had been trying to tell me all along.

Given the cultural continuum and the great diversity of economic opportunities, it is impossible to show two-way correlations between ethnicity and economics with my 130-household sample. The existence of the cultural continuum itself, and the way it relates to economic variables, can be seen in the tables in Chapters Five and Six, although statistically significant correlations cannot be shown for these relationships. The ethnic traits used in these tables are derived from my analysis of field notes on key informant interviews and participant observation. A fuller discussion of these ethnic traits is found in Chapter Three.

Each of the three methods discussed here has its limitations and its usefulness. In combination, they provide checks on each other as well as yielding different kinds of data that can contribute to an overall picture not elicited by any of the methods alone. This synthesis can then be interpreted with a certain amount of confidence that the basis, if not the interpretation itself, is sound.

1

History of the Mayo Region

Introduction

The Mayo valley today is one of the most modern areas in Mexico, controlled by wealthy farmers whose values coincide with those of mainstream Mexican society. Less than 100 years ago this valley was largely controlled by the Mayo Indians, whose culture, while substantially hispanicized, was quite distinct from that of the non-Indian population of the region. The history of the valley is a key to how the Mayos retained control of their territory for so long and how they lost that control after, as they thought, they had won the battle to keep it. The long history of the Mayos' military resistance to outside control, as well as their important role as allies of certain political factions in Sonoran and Mexican power struggles, point up rather vividly the irony of the present-day circumstances of the descendants of Totoliguoqui. Furthermore, the history of Mayo resistance is an important aspect of the underlying ethnic conflicts that still exist in many communities in the valley, despite the ostensible submission of Mayo descendants to the bearers of the national culture.

The Mayos and Spanish Contact

The earliest Spanish expeditions, in 1532 and 1534, into what is now northwest Mexico and southern Arizona, skirted the *Cáhita*[1] area, staying in the Sierra Madre Occidental to the east. The hostility of the natives of the coast was one reason for the sierra route, but the Spanish were also looking for mines and were often guided by natives who were enemies of the Yaquis

---

1. Cáhita is a term used by anthropologists to describe both Mayo and Yaqui culture and language, as well as the geographical area where these two groups live (see Beals 1945). In the Mayo language, the word cáhita means "there is none."

and the peoples living upriver from the Mayos. Because of this more popular route, contact between the Spanish and Mayos did not occur until 1585. In that year, Hernando de Bazán arrived with an army at the Mayo river. The Mayos received him peacefully, but he put some of them in chains, thus initiating the ambivalent relations between Mayos and the bearers of European culture ever since (Alegre 1841, vol. 1:362; Dabdoub 1970:41).

Although the Mayos did engage in armed resistance against Spanish and later Mestizo residents of the Mayo region, historical records show that in general they were less warlike than most of their neighbors (Alegre 1841, vol. 1:362, vol. 2:204, 325; Pérez de Ribas 1645:236, 238). It may have been in order to gain military advantage that in 1614 the Mayos allied with the Spanish army against the Yaquis and other neighboring groups. In return, they were given horses and promised the protection of the Spanish army (Alegre, vol. 2:204). In the same year, the Mayos requested that a Spanish priest be sent to christianize them. Padre Pedro Méndez, a Jesuit, was sent for this purpose and was welcomed by Mayo leaders even before reaching the first hamlet (Pérez de Ribas, p. 239). Méndez, in a letter to Pérez de Ribas (pp. 239-240), comments on how much more willing were the Mayos than their neighbors to be baptized and to follow the rules of the Church. By 1620, all the Mayos had been baptized; at that time they numbered approximately 30,000 (ibid., p. 249).

It was during the period of Jesuit rule in the Mayo region that the culture of this group changed and crystallized into the syncretic system whose autonomy the Mayos defended for over a hundred years. The Jesuits consolidated a loosely federated group of scattered hamlets into seven *pueblos*, each with its own elected governor and *mayordomo*. The Jesuits also introduced wheat and cattle, enabling the Mayos to produce a surplus for the first time. The Mayos' acceptance of the Catholic religion, so enthusiastically reported by the missionaries, was evidently not so complete as they may have wished. Many clearly aboriginal elements of ritual and belief remain in the contemporary religious system; either these were allowed by the Jesuits to coexist with orthodox aspects of the Catholic faith, or aboriginal beliefs and practices remained alive outside the accepted ritual system and were reintegrated after the Jesuits were removed from the scene, in 1767, by order of the Spanish Crown.

In any event, Mayo culture at the time of the Jesuits' departure was neither the aboriginal one nor that of the Spanish, but one that combined elements from both into an integrated political, economic, and religious system (Hu-DeHart 1984:4). Thus, unlike the Indian cultures of Mesoamerica, the culture which resulted from contact was not one that isolated communities and subordinated them to the Spanish hierarchy, both political and religious (see Smith 1977:11-12; Friedlander 1975:xiv). Rather, the system organized under Jesuit rule served to unite politically a previously scattered group, to provide this group with the means to produce surplus food, and to create a religious system in which a priest is not necessary. To be sure, the Jesuits were not entirely altruistic in their actions, and the system they helped to bring about served their own purposes very well. However, for over a hundred years after their expulsion no one--not the Church and not the military--could manage to establish the control over the Indians which the Jesuits had enjoyed for most of their time in Sonora.

The Spanish Colonial Period

At the time of the Spanish conquest of Mexico, the bulk of the indigenous population was to be found in the southern areas, and complex state societies were prevalent there. This was not the case in the northwest, where even the Yaquis, the most populous group, never developed a political hierarchy or an economic elite (Hu-DeHart 1984:4). The fact that the Mayos were not accustomed to paying tribute or to obeying political leaders made them unsuitable for the often exploitive *encomienda* system prevalent in the more densely populated regions of the new colony. The Jesuits were given a fairly free hand with the Mayos, and although the assumption was that pacification of the Indians would be complete in 10 years, in fact the Jesuits controlled the Mayo and Yaqui territories for more than 150 years.

The Jesuits persuaded the Mayos to produce surplus food and other products, portraying the export of these items as exchanges for the improved lifestyle provided by the priests. Although their system was certainly a form of tribute, the Jesuits were in general less extractive than their secular counterparts to the south. The priests introduced cattle raising as well as wheat and other new crops, and these were very successful: food was exported from the Mayo valley as far as the missions of California and Arizona. Indeed, it was the surplus from the Mayo and Yaqui valleys that made possible the founding of these more northern missions.

In addition to economic change, the Jesuits also brought about political changes that later made possible the military organization necessary for successful resistance to outside encroachment. Before the advent of the Spanish, the Mayos lived in dispersed hamlets and evidently had no political hierarchy. By congregating the population into villages and introducing the concept of elected political leadership, the Jesuits could supervise the missions and extract tribute more efficiently. Of course, this concentration also introduced the idea of hierarchical organization and allegiance to political leaders. These two elements were crucial to later military resistance and almost certainly contributed to the maintenance of Mayo culture into the 20th century.

The first truly violent Mayo resistance occurred in 1740. Before 1734, Sonora had been ruled by military commandants who were subject politically to the government of the province of Nueva Vizcaya. In that year, Sonora and Sinaloa were combined to form a province in its own right, ruled by Manuel Bernal de Huidobro (Bancroft 1884:520). This political change indicates an increasing interest in the area on the part of the Spanish. Pacification of the natives was seen as almost complete, and Spanish settlers, especially those with mining interests in the silver-rich sierras, wished to take advantage of the newly available work force. This required disengaging the Indians from the missions, and the Spanish encouraged the Mayos to press for secularization (ibid., p. 522). At the same time, the new provincial government had begun to demand taxes from the Sonoran Indians; it also demanded that each pueblo give up a portion of land. Governor Huidobro accused the Jesuits of wanting absolute power over the Indians, to the point of refusing to allow them to work in the mines and newly established haciendas despite the wishes of secular Spanish settlers and the Mayos themselves in this regard (Hu-DeHart 1984:14-15; 1981:60). To these bases of conflict among the Spanish, the Indians added complaints of being overworked and of not receiving adequate compensation for their efforts (Hu-DeHart 1981:67).

With this uneasy situation as a setting, the Mayo governor was mysteriously killed in 1740. Combined with heavy floods and a resulting famine, these events led to an armed uprising by the Mayos, who eventually joined the Yaquis and almost every other indigenous group in Sonora in what became a full-scale revolt that many Spanish feared would result in an all-out race war (Hu-DeHart 1984:16). At the height of the uprising, the combined forces controlled all of present-day southwestern Sonora and had caused all non-Indians, except the prisoners of war, to abandon the region. It was only with the arrival of Spanish reinforcements, in August of 1740, that the Indians were defeated. Their surrender began in September and was complete by November, when Governor Huidobro left the mining city of Alamos, where he had taken refuge during the war.

The 1741 Treaty of Alamos, which guaranteed amnesty and political autonomy to Mayos and Yaquis, does not indicate that the rebels were entirely defeated (Dabdoub 1970:88-95; Alegre 1841, vol. 4:391-394). The revolt of 1740 did, however, mark the beginning of a long period of Spanish encroachment and Mayo resistance in which the Mayos gradually lost all the rights guaranteed by that treaty.

By 1740, Spanish civilians had already established some haciendas in Mayo territory, although there is no record of how many. The Spanish government had built forts at Alamos, in the sierra above the Mayo valley, and at Santa Cruz, near the mouth of the Mayo river. The Yaquis, who enjoyed greater autonomy and who controlled the sierra at the time of this first uprising, have managed to retain or regain most of the political autonomy and land rights that the Mayos have lost. Thus, the 1740 date is important in marking not only the first Mayo uprising but also the divergence between Mayos and Yaquis which has interested present-day scholars (cf. Beals 1945:211-215; Spicer 1970:113-124; Hu-DeHart 1984:227).

The conditions that sparked the 1740 uprising were not eliminated by it. In the years immediately following, Jesuit control of the Mayo region declined constantly as the Mayos resolutely left the missions to work in the mines of the Spanish Crown. It is doubtful that the Indians wished to be liberated from mission life entirely; in fact, during the 1740 uprising they were reported as continuing in their religious devotions despite the absence of the missionaries. Their desire for the independence to be derived from wages earned in the mines, as well as for the liberating experience of traveling beyond their native land, is quite understandable, however.

In spite of the wishes of both the Jesuits and the Mayos to keep some form of the mission system, Spanish officials supported the secularization of the Mayo and Yaqui missions (Hu-DeHart 1981:88-89), thereby opening both regions to Spanish settlers and making available to them the large labor pool represented by the Indians. It was the staunch resistance of the Jesuits not only to secularization but to the employment of mission Indians in the mines that led ultimately to the expulsion of the order from all Spanish American territory in 1767.

With the expulsion of the Jesuits there began the process of partitioning the area formerly controlled by them in trust for the Mayos. Although the rule of the missionaries was somewhat autocratic and did not always serve the interests of the Indians, these interests gradually became less and less important to those who came to rule the region.

One of the first acts of the Spanish after expelling the Jesuits was to confiscate all mission property and secularize all Mayo missions (Pinart n.d., 4th ser., vol. 2:212-213). The consequences of this act were immediate and, for the most part, negative for the Mayos. The military ruler of the area placed the mission churches under the supervision of secular commissaries pending the arrival of new priests (ibid.), but these caretakers evidently allowed the missions to deteriorate beyond rehabilitation. Although officially the former mission lands and the goods associated with the churches were to be handed over to secular priests, in fact the few priests who were assigned to the former missions did not have access to these lands nor to the money that had been paid by the government to the Jesuits (Reyes 1784 in Tovar Pinzón 1971: 57; Revilla Gigedo 1794). A report to the King of Spain by the Bishop of Sonora in 1784 indicates that two of the three missions in the Mayo valley were in ruins, and the third badly damaged. The priests were demoralized and the Indians lived dispersed away from their villages, neglecting their crops and livestock (Reyes in Tovar Pinzón, pp. 69-71). A second report, in 1794, from the Viceroy, states that the missions in the Mayo region were "without priests, without churches, and without the commons (*bienes de la comunidad*), which were dissipated by the royal commissaries" (Revilla Gigedo 1794).

As with its decrees on the fate of the missions, the government made very specific stipulations as to the disposition of lands in the hands of the Indians themselves and formerly protected by Jesuit control. In 1769, José de

Gálvez, *Visitador General*, gave instructions for the distribution of these lands, along with titles to them, to specific families of Indians. Although his instructions indicate that the Indians themselves should be allowed to participate in this distribution, the amount of land to be allotted to each pueblo was limited to 4 leagues square (32 square miles), with some exceptions. These instructions also provided for the granting of land to Spanish military personnel in the region. Most important for the history of the Mayo valley, Gálvez stipulated that all other lands be given to Spaniards and *gente de razón* (i.e., nonpeninsular Mestizos), thereby legitimizing the influx of outsiders into the Mayo valley. At one stroke, the Mayos were deprived of most of their tribal homeland, which was officially opened to Mestizos. In addition to the distribution of lands, Gálvez ordered that each Indian pay tribute to the Crown, a first for the Mayos, who were exempt from tribute under Jesuit rule (Pinart, 3rd ser., vol. 4:708-712).

It is probable that not all of Gálvez' orders were carried out as thoroughly as they were stated; however, the provision of legal means for hacendados to acquire lands in the area opened a door previously closed to them. Indeed, by 1784 there were already Spanish and Mestizo settlers in every Mayo pueblo, occupying lands previously worked by the Indians (Reyes in Tovar Pinzón, pp. 69-71). Conditions in the Mayo valley were certainly not improved by whatever governmental actions were taken. Viceroy Revilla Gigedo's 1794 report paints a rather dreary picture of the region 27 years after the expulsion of the Jesuits:

> The flight of entire families, or their voluntary and irremediable move to the hills, and other places, left the villages almost without people and without government, without police, the churches deserted, and fields without arms to work them or to tend the cattle, which are like skeletons. . . .

This report contrasts sharply with Hu-DeHart's (1981:99-103) descriptions of life in the nearby Yaqui region after the departure of the Jesuits. Her view is that the Yaquis went to the hills to work as miners, that their churches were maintained, and that agriculture flourished during this period. Indeed, it is her contention that the long history of Yaqui cultural maintenance began with the independence they enjoyed in the post-Jesuit era. Although Mayos may have worked in the mines surrounding the city of Alamos, there is no evidence that they prospered thereby, and the cultural and social cohesion that Hu-DeHart postulates for postmissionary Yaqui society is not to be found documented in any of the historical literature on the Mayos. Rather than encouraging cultural stability and resistance to outsiders, the events of the latter part of the 18th century worked against the Mayos. It is clear that the tide of encroachment against which they had rebelled in 1740 became a flood after the expulsion of the Jesuits. With the help of their Yaqui neighbors to the north, the Mayos spent much of the 19th century attempting, ultimately without success, to turn back this tide.

The period from 1767 until Mexican independence in 1821 was peaceful in the sense that no major armed rebellions took place in the Mayo area, despite the fact that Gálvez had in 1769 set up local militias with Mayo leaders (Navarro García 1964:175). The disintegration of the mission structure and the dispersal of the natives evidently made impossible the organization necessary for revolt. Mayos and Sonorans in general participated only marginally in the War for Independence (1808-1821), and indeed Sonora kept more or less aloof from national politics throughout the 19th century.

The Long Struggle for Autonomy

Sonora's detachment from national affairs was brought about at least in part by the intense internal political turmoil that characterized the state in this period. This turmoil was augmented by almost continual raids from Apaches in the north, by incursions from American, French, and British "filibusters," and by Mayo and Yaqui resistance to ever-increasing Mestizo encroachment on tribal lands. At this time, Sonoran politics were entirely in the hands of the Mestizos, descendants of Spanish settlers, who regarded themselves as the rightful owners of Sonoran lands and mines (Acuña 1974:50). From the point of view of the Mayos, the period consisted of a series of Mestizo encroachments alternating with Mayo resistance, by force of arms. This protracted war of attrition gradually eroded Mayo autonomy in the valley, although the Mayos and Yaquis scored many victories in the course of their struggle for political and economic independence.

Mexican independence from Spain in 1821 brought few changes in local politics in the Mayo region. The Indians, who had expected to be given voting privileges and local autonomy, remained officially under the control of the Mestizos (Hardy 1829:439-440). In 1825, under the leadership of Juan Banderas, the Yaquis rose up in arms and were later joined by the Mayos. The Yaqui rebellion was directly related to the imposition of Mestizo military leaders: the Yaquis refused to comply with a Mestizo order to mobilize forces to combat the Apaches in the north. The Mestizo reaction to this was to occupy the Yaqui village of Ráum. This signaled the beginning of a rebellion that eventually spread from the Fuerte river in Sinaloa to Ures in the north of Sonora. Banderas claimed that he only wanted justice, which he saw as complete autonomy for Yaquis and Mayos. He sent a commission to Mexico City offering to disband when the government agreed to respect the rights of the Indians. In 1827 Banderas, having been assured of the position of Captain General of the Yaquis and Mayos, agreed to lay down his arms, and in 1828 the government passed a series of decrees ostensibly settling the dispute.

A closer inspection of these decrees reveals that the government took away with one hand the autonomy it appeared to give with the other. The first decree guaranteed amnesty to all Yaqui and Mayo rebels and granted citizenship to all the Indians in the region. However, this decree also abolished all-Indian militias, as well as the title of Captain General so recently conferred on Banderas. The second decree provided for the political and economic integration of the two valleys into the national system. This law also placed political authority over the disputed regions in the hands of non-Indians, and provided tax and land incentives for them to settle in these regions. The third decree required all Indians to live in their communities rather than dispersed or in the mountains (Hu-DeHart 1984:32-36).

Clearly, these decrees do not represent a victory for the Indians. On the other hand, the inability of the government to implement them established a pattern that prevailed for most of the 19th century. The lack of personnel to adjudicate land claims, the active resistance of the Mayos and Yaquis themselves to the implementation of these laws, and the severe lack of military manpower to enforce them combined to secure the essential failure of the decrees of 1828.

In understanding the failure of the government to implement these and subsequent measures to subdue the Indians, the environment of the region must be taken into account. The entire state of Sonora is remote from the more densely populated central region where Mexico City lies. Sonora is also separated from neighboring Chihuahua by the Sierra Madre mountain chain. Combined with this isolation was a sparse non-Indian population and the fierce climate of the region itself. Although the population of "gente de razón" increased over time, it was until recently vastly outnumbered by Indians, who were in addition more used to the hellish climatic conditions of their homeland. The natural vegetation, aptly named "thorn forest," is composed of a dense array of cacti and other thorny plants, which makes it necessary for horses as well as their riders to wear thick leather coverings for protection. The temperature regularly soars to well over 100 degrees Fahrenheit, and the heavy rains in the mountains during the summer make for deadly flash floods. The Spanish and later Mestizo Mexicans who moved into this area were at a disadvantage in not being prepared to deal with these conditions. The Indians had the further leverage of being on home turf. These advantages, combined with a fierce determination and brilliant military leadership, made it possible for the combined Yaqui and Mayo forces to resist the Sonoran army for the entire 19th century.

Indeed, so helpless was the government of Sonora that in 1831 it accepted proposals by the Indians to reinstate the all-Indian militias, with Indian officers, and to allow the election of Indians as local leaders. Despite this capitulation by the government, Mestizo encroachment was not completely undermined and, depending on how the tides of battle turned, continued throughout this period.

It was Mestizo attempts to rig the election of Mayo leaders in July of 1831 that set the stage for the next rebellion, in 1832. The Mestizo authorities wished to impose a malleable Mayo as Captain General, but Mayos declared their own candidate to have won the most votes. After a visit to Banderas in the Yaqui valley, Mayo leaders agreed to negotiate with authorities and ultimately accepted an alternate man as Captain General. The Mestizo authorities, clearly misjudging their strength, responded to the peaceful settlement of a potentially volatile situation by denouncing the Mayo leaders. The Mestizos called for the punishment of the Indians and issued an order for the arrest of Banderas.

The Mestizo attempt to impose political and military leaders on the Mayos was only one incitement to resistance. Another was the encroachment of Mestizos from the town of Alamos on land in the Mayo village of Camoa. The deaf ear turned on Mayo complaints about these land claims caused the Mayos of that pueblo also to ask Banderas' help. The combined political and economic acts of hubris on the part of the Mestizos prompted Banderas to march to the Mayo region, and a full-scale rebellion was once again under way.

The 1832 rebellion, like that of 1825, spread far to the north of Yaqui and Mayo territory. However, by the fall of 1832, having run out of supplies and energy, Banderas apparently allowed himself to be captured near the northern town of Arizpe. He was executed in 1833 (Hu-DeHart 1984:37-47). Banderas' death did not spell the end of the uprising, however, for his followers continued the revolt for another nine months, after which the new Yaqui leader maintained an armed peace in southern Sonora (Bancroft 1884:656-659).

While the Indians were reacting violently to government and private encroachment on their power and territory, the Mestizos themselves were embroiled in constant conflict over control of the state government. The years following the Banderas revolts featured a political rivalry between José Urrea and Manuel María Gándara; this conflict was loosely connected with the national struggle between Centralists and Federalists, but revolved more closely around state and local issues and allegiances. Gándara, after first joining the Federalist forces, switched to centralism, encouraging the Mayos and Yaquis to support him. This they did during his entire career as Sonoran *caudillo*. That Gándara could count on the support of the Mayos is ironic, because he consistently represented the interests of the landed oligarchy, the same element whose encroachment had provoked Banderas and earlier rebels. It was certainly to the landowners' advantage to appear favorable to the Indians' interests. Without the labor of Mayos and Yaquis on the haciendas and in the mines, those enterprises could never have been successful. Indeed, even at the height of the Indian wars, hacendados were reluctant to turn over rebellious workers to authorities, despite the fact that haciendas were usually the targets of Indian attacks.

In any event, Gándara evidently managed to exploit the Indians' fear of encroachment and the loss of their land in order to gain their support against Urrea. Urrea's ill-timed attempt, in 1842, to implement the decrees of 1828, calling for the distribution of Mayo and Yaqui land to Mestizos (Hu-DeHart 1984:60-62) helped Gándara's cause considerably. After several years of fighting between Urrea and Gándara, a shaky peace was established in 1846, under Gándara's rule. The Indians, however, remained dissatisfied with the outcome of the conflict because they received no assurances of the autonomy they sought (Bancroft 1884:660-661; 663).

Gándara's political success had depended on his favoring the wealthy landholding class and on his popularity with the Indians. However, by the 1850s the increasing number of merchants and miners had become dissatisfied with Gándara, and a coalition supporting José de Aguilar and Ignacio Pesqueira emerged from the chaos of Sonoran politics. After several political maneuvers, the conflict between the two segments of the Mestizo population became violent, and Pesqueira, with the support of the citizens of Alamos, defeated Gándara in 1857.

This victory and the continuing support of Alameños for Pesqueira highlight the nature of the struggle in terms of the Mayo area. The Alameños wanted to gain control of the rich lands of the Mayo valley; these lands were all the more desirable given that Alamos' isolation and the difficulty of transporting bullion on bandit-plagued highways were causing a decline in the grandeur of that once elegant city. Pesqueira promised in 1858 to allow Alameños to begin colonies in the Yaqui and Mayo valleys and to open the port of Santa Cruz on the Mayo river. In the same year, Pesqueira forcefully put down the remaining Mayo rebels and issued orders requiring the Indians to have licenses to bear arms, on penalty of imprisonment. Despite these rulings, Mayos and Yaquis rebelled in 1859 and 1860, again in protest against Mestizo encroachments that had been encouraged by Pesqueira. Pesqueira had left the state during this period in order to fight on the Liberal side in the national War of Reform, led by Benito Juárez. His absence was blamed for the Indian uprisings and eventually cost him the support of the Alameños (Acuña 1974:42, 46-48, 51, 65).

Subsequent Mayo revolts, in 1861 and 1862, were put down by troops from Alamos, not by Pesqueira's army. That army suffered a humiliating defeat at the hands of the French interventionists at Guaymas in 1864 (Corral 1959:40-42, 50). This defeat, followed by several others, triggered uprisings by the Mayos and other Indians. Conservative forces led by Gándara again aspired to control Sonora, in the name of Maximillian's empire. In 1865 Pesqueira, having lost the Sonoran capital, retreated to Arizona, and French forces took power in Sonora. One of the strongholds of the pro-empire faction was Alamos, which had now become violently anti-Pesqueira.

The Indians, already enraged by Pesqueira's fostering of Mestizo settlement of the Yaqui and Mayo valleys (Hu-DeHart 1984:84-85), were persuaded by promises of autonomy to join the Conservative faction. The

Mayos, who had fought against Alamos troops in 1862, became the mainstay of the army loyal to the empire in 1865 (Corral 1959:53-54; Acuña 1974:88). This army, led by José María Tranquilino Almada, defended Alamos against Republican forces from Sinaloa in 1865, but was driven into the Mayo valley and defeated in 1866. This signaled the turn in the imperialists' fortunes which eventually ended in complete defeat in September of that year (Acuña, pp. 91-92). The remaining French troops withdrew from Sonora, leaving their former allies at the mercy of the Republicans (Bancroft 1884:697). The Mayos remained loyal to the empire to the very end, and the last battle of the war in Sonora took place at Alamos, under the leadership of Almada. After his defeat, Almada was executed and Pesqueira once again took political control of Sonora (Acuña, pp. 92-93).

The defeat of the imperialists did not end Mayo resistance, however, and its continuation demonstrates that Mayo interests were only tenuously linked to those of conservative Sonorans. After the defeat of the empire, Mestizo migration to the valley resumed (Sonora 1913:19-20), and so did Mayo protests against it (Acuña, p. 99). In 1867 the Mayos became active in their resistance, and in the same year the Yaquis attacked three Mayo pueblos and killed the Mayo leaders who opposed military action (ibid.; Corral 1900:73). The following year, Mayos killed several Mestizo residents of the pueblos of Santa Cruz, Etchojoa, San Pedro, and Agiabampo, making off with cattle and household goods from their haciendas and stores (Corral 1900:52).

The government forces during this period, led by General Jesús García Morales, were particularly brutal in their battles against the Indians. In 1868, these battles took on more the character of massacres of innocents. The troops evidently rode through the Mayo territory wantonly killing unarmed men, taking the women and children prisoner, and confiscating all the cattle and other possessions of the Indians. A commander of state troops locked over 400 Indians in a church in the Yaqui pueblo of Bácum. During the night the troops opened fire with artillery upon their defenseless captives. When the shooting stopped, only 59 people remained alive in the church, and although many had escaped, there were 120 Indian dead. Only one government soldier was killed (Corral 1900:52-53; Acuña 1974:100).

In May of that year the soldiers left the Mayo region, and in July Mayos attacked the pueblos of Etchojoa and Santa Cruz. This siege was stopped only because the river inundated all the communities on its banks in the worst flood ever recorded in the valley. The government responded to the violence by building three new forts in the Yaqui and Mayo valleys (Corral 1959:74). At this time the Mestizos once again began migrating to the Mayo valley, establishing new haciendas and implementing irrigation works. The newcomers looked hungrily at the territory still in Mayo hands and became determined to take it over at all costs. Writing in the 1880s, Ramon Corral (1959:200) reports:

There exists there a great, unexploited source of rich and varied products, which only needs the pacification of the tribes and the hard work of civilized man to bear abundant fruit and to change the face of the state.

The Mayos, however, saw these lands with different eyes. They demonstrated their determination to maintain their now-eroded control of the valley and regain lost autonomy by raiding haciendas and pueblos in the hands of Mestizos and, from 1875 to 1888, by participating in the now legendary wars under the leadership of José María Leyva, commonly known as Cajeme (Corral 1959:118).

A Yaqui who had spent most of his life among Mestizos and had considerable military experience, Cajeme was named leader of the Yaqui and Mayo tribes in 1874 as a reward for supporting Pesqueira in the war against the French (Acuña 1974:122-123). The Indian leader then moved to consolidate his power in both valleys. He reorganized the local government, appointing Indians loyal to him as pueblo leaders. He maintained a militia from taxes, and later from the spoils of battle, and he bought arms and ammunition secretly in Guaymas (Corral 1959:196).

In 1884, an observer noted that the Mayos and Yaquis controlled the land they occupied, and that Cajeme could have carried out a war of extermination had he wanted more than power over the traditional tribal territory. Even that territory, at least in the Mayo valley, had become seriously reduced by the 1870s: Navojoa, one of the seven original Mayo pueblos, had been designated as head of a Mexican *municipio*[2] in 1861 (Hu-DeHart 1984:83), and in 1905 was described as on the border of the Mayo tribe (Troncoso 1905:26). Navojoa became the target for many Mayo attacks during the 1875-88 wars, and the Mestizo troops organized there rather than at Alamos, the center for all previous Mestizo movements (Corral 1959:207-208).

The Cajeme wars began with general unrest in both valleys in 1875-76, with the Mayos burning Mestizo haciendas as well as the town of Santa Cruz (Acuña 1974:126). In 1877 the Mayos encountered the Navojoa cavalry. The Mayos were defeated, but Mestizos began abandoning the valley in fear (Corral 1959:206). In 1880 the state legislature, faced with Apache attacks and a civil war between José Pesqueira and Francisco Serna as well as the Cajeme revolt, asked for federal troops to occupy the Yaqui and Mayo valleys. The refusal of this request gave encouragement to Cajeme. In 1882 the Navojoa Mestizos, led by the military commander of Alamos, began organizing an army. In October of that year Cajeme arrived in Etchojoa with 2,000 Yaquis and was joined by 1,000 Mayos. At this point all Mestizos except for the militia had abandoned the valley, and only 500 armed men

---

2. A municipio is an area with an elected leadership, similar to a county in the United States.

remained in Navojoa. The state of alarm continued throughout 1883. In 1884, independently of Cajeme, Mayos marched on Navojoa and began a siege that lasted two months. A temporary truce was called at the end of that year (ibid., pp. 211-212).

In 1885, Cajeme's house was burned and he called for armed protest. Both Mayos and Yaquis attacked and burned several towns, and 1,000 Mayos occupied the village of Masiaca and began fortifying it and other pueblos in their possession. These actions finally persuaded the federal government to send troops to the region. In 1886, there were more than 100 battles between Indians and government troops. In October, Cajeme volunteered to stop fighting if the soldiers agreed to leave the valleys, but this offer was turned down. At the end of the year 1,600 Mayos and 4,000 Yaquis had been captured, and many were becoming disheartened by the wars. Cajeme was captured and killed; his death marked defeat for the Indians. Although both Mayos and Yaquis continued fighting, many abandoned the valleys for the sierra (Troncoso 1905:108-158). These people began to return to their homelands in the following year, though Yaqui guerrilla activity continued from bases in the sierra.

In the Mayo valley, peace was restored in 1888. At this time, a politico-religious movement began to grow up around Teresa Urrea, a girl from the sierra town of Cabora, who had acquired a reputation as a healer and later as a saint. Miraculous cures were attributed to her, and she also made speeches inciting the people to fight for their land. A special liturgy, combining aspects of Catholicism with political rhetoric and new rituals, was practiced at Teresa's father's ranch near Cabora. Coming at a time of economic and political turmoil resulting from the national government's policies, Teresa's combination of religious revivalism and political zeal evidently held widespread appeal for the victims of those policies, among whom the Mayos may be counted. In 1892, Mayo troops, shouting "Long live the saint of Cabora," again captured Navojoa and killed the Mestizo leaders. In July of that year Teresa and her father were deported to Arizona, where they remained until their deaths. Teresa continued as a cult figure and curer, inspiring a raid by Yaquis on Nogales, Sonora in 1896 (Gill 1960).

Loosely connected with the Teresa Urrea movement, and more peaceful than the attack on Navojoa, a millenarian movement also developed among the Mayos at this time. In September of 1890 there was a large meeting of Mayos at which men and women called "saints" gave long speeches. These saints predicted the end of the world, after which Mayo authority would be restored in the valley. God, it was said, was about to send a flood to destroy the Mestizos. This meeting and others like it in subsequent years were peaceful, but were disbanded by the Mestizo military commander, who took the saints prisoner (Troncoso 1905:176-185).

Spicer (1970) characterizes Mayo behavior after 1890 as passive in comparison with that before this date and with the Yaqui militarism following it. He suggests that the greater extent of Mestizo infiltration in the

Mayo valley and the consequent gradual erosion of Mayo autonomy were the cause of the Mayos' interest in passive nativism characterized by the millenarian movement of 1890. It is certainly true, as Spicer says, that Mestizo infiltration was much greater in the Mayo than in the Yaqui region; it is also true that the Mayo saints' speeches were pacifistic and represent the classic millenarian movement's dependence on divine intervention rather than practical action in the face of relative deprivation. It is not strictly true, however, that the Mayos were peaceful after 1890, or even after the 1892 capture of Navojoa. Although less consistently active than the Yaquis, the Mayos continued to ally themselves militarily with those who promised them autonomy and the return of their lands. They were simply hoodwinked into fighting a war in which they were the losers even though their faction won.

Peons and Revolutionaries

If Sonorans stayed out of national politics for most of the 19th century, they came to dominate the national political scene for the better part of the 20th. It was by manipulating national politics and finances, in fact, that Sonoran Mestizos finally conquered the Mayos and took control of the fertile lands they had coveted for so long.

The history of the years 1890-1910 in the Mayo region is marked by the resumption of Mestizo inroads into Mayo territory. This encroachment had ceased and indeed been reversed during the Cajeme wars, but now it was resumed under the protection of the government of President Porfirio Díaz. Díaz' main interest was to civilize the country through massive importation of foreign technology and knowhow. During his regime, the railway between Nogales, Sonora and Mazatlán, Sinaloa was built, with Navojoa an important station. Between 1892 and 1902, 18 canals were constructed along the Mayo river; these canals irrigated the vast haciendas that were carved out of former tribal lands and represented the realization of Mestizo dreams for the development of the region. Sonora now became an example of the kind of progress that could be achieved with technological advances and the availability of cheap labor (Aguilar 1977:31-32).

By 1900, the Mestizos had established firm control over the former Mayo territory. The pueblos had been incorporated into state municipios with Mestizo leaders. The three municipios with the bulk of the Mayo population--Etchojoa, Huatabampo, and Navojoa--had in 1900 over 35,000 hectares of land in Mestizo hands (Ulloa 1900:141-142, 144-145). This land was worked by the Mayos, who had become peons in their own homeland. The Mestizo town of Huatabampo replaced the original pueblo of Santa Cruz, destroyed during the Cajeme wars, as the predominant urban center in the lower Mayo valley.

The Porfiriato marks the low point in Mayo-Mestizo relations. Mayo lands were seized at an unprecedented rate, and the Indians were subjected by force and trickery to the kind of debt peonage common in other parts of

Mexico but heretofore unknown in Sonora. The infamous *rurales*, government agents, occupied the area as an invading army, and Mestizos claimed tribal lands with impunity. The official position of the Díaz regime was that Indians were racially inferior and suited only for manual labor under the direction of Whites.

This policy was carried out ruthlessly in the Mayo valley, where foreigners were given land if they promised to populate the region with outsiders in order to improve the genetic makeup of the population (Medina 1941). The lands that the Alameños and others had coveted for so long finally came into their hands. Migrants also came from other states to take advantage of the availability of new land: between 1884 and 1910 the population of the municipio of Navojoa grew from 1,334 to 10,882. The majority of the migrants settled in the area around Huatabampo and Etchojoa, formerly controlled by the Mayos (Aguilar 1977:19). Meanwhile, the Mayos suffered silently and awaited their chance to respond.

It was in this context of major social and economic changes that Alvaro Obregón, future leader of the Revolution, was born and raised. The last of 18 children, Obregón was born in 1880 at Siquisiva, near Navojoa, into a family whose fortunes had been declining for 40 years. His father died three months after Alvaro's birth, leaving the family dependent on the relatives of Alvaro's mother, Cenobia Salido. The Salido family, fortunately for the young Obregón, had been among the first to move into the lower valley, and owned several extensive haciendas near Huatabampo. In 1898 the Obregón family moved to that town, where Alvaro attended school. While still in school, he worked as a mechanic in a carriage shop and in the flour mill of one of his uncles; by age 20 he had gained a reputation as an expert mechanic, especially with agricultural machinery. He took advantage of his knowledge by applying it cautiously but successfully on a 150-hectare farm, located near Huatabampo, which he purchased from the Díaz government in 1905 and subsequently expanded as his fortunes rose (Bojórquez 1929:13).

Although Alvaro had little time during this period to devote to revolutionary activities, his brother José and his nephew Benjamin Hill were involved in clandestine political meetings in Navojoa from 1907 to 1910. In 1910, Francisco Madero proclaimed the beginning of the Revolution, and in 1911 José Obregón was named Provisional President of the Municipio of Huatabampo. The following year, Alvaro was elected to that office (Bojórquez 1929:14), from which he launched his political and military career.

From the very beginning of this career, Alvaro Obregón depended for his success on the Mayo Indians. His election as Municipal President of Huatabampo was declared valid only after his opponent's challenge to the eligibility of the Mayos to vote was dismissed by the state legislature (Hall 1981:25). Thus it was Mayo votes that first put him in political office. One of his first acts in office was to eliminate the tax on irrigation canals (Hall 1981:26), thereby reducing construction costs and facilitating encroachment on

Descendants of Totoliguoqui

Indian lands. He also added to the funds available for rural schools, evidently in an attempt to integrate the rural Mayo population into the national culture.

The years 1912-14 saw the Mayo revolt under Miguel Totoliguoqui, who had led the 1892 attack on Navojoa (Gill 1960:23). The Indians destroyed buildings in several towns, killing the Mestizo residents. The revolt ended when Totoliguoqui was killed in 1914, near the village of Júpare. Officially, Totoliguoqui and his troops were part of the war between the Maytorenistas and the Villistas, two of the revolutionary factions opposing Díaz. However, it is clear that the goal of the Mayos was the return of their land, not the national struggle for power (Almada 1971:201).

It was by winning that struggle that Obregón attained his goal of developing the Mayo valley. From 1912 until his death, the context of Obregón's career became increasingly national and less clearly local. It also was for the most part as a military leader that he lived his life, although he always saw himself as a civilian at heart (Hall 1981:37). His brilliant military successes in Sonora against Orozco and later in the national Constitutionalist war depended first and last on the legendary strength and bravery of the Mayos and Yaquis who were his troops.

It may be said, therefore, that from the point of view of Porfirio Díaz and later Victoriano Huerta, the Mayos were not at peace. From the Mayo point of view, also, there was little difference in the objectives of their fighting: political autonomy and the return of their tribal lands were always the goals of the Indians, whether as allies of Gándara or the French or as autonomous warriors. Aguilar (1977:374) states about the Yaquis, who joined the Constitutionalists in 1914, that they "fought the *federales* because they had always been their enemies." The same can be said for the Mayos: they fought in the Revolution because the revolutionaries promised to return their lands and autonomy. These promises, inevitably, were empty, at least in the case of the Mayos.

It was as the leader of a national constituency, attained by virtue of his charismatic military leadership, that Obregón finally achieved the transfer of Mayo territory into the hands of the national government and private, primarily Mestizo, landowners. What Sonorans alone had failed to attain during more than a century of bloodshed, Obregón and his Sonoran allies succeeded in bringing about peacefully in the matter of a few years. Obregón was instrumental in the writing and implementation of the Mexican Constitution (Hall 1981:167), which, as interpreted by his allies in the Sonoran government, paved the way for the distribution of Mayo lands. This betrayal has not been lost on the Mayos. In 1978, a Mayo who had fought under Obregón and had been among those who entered Mexico City triumphantly in 1914, ahead of all the other Constitutionalists, had this to say about the leader:

> Here [in the Mayo valley] they raised up the people with the promise that, upon winning, they were going to give them the land. In that respect, he [Obregón] did not fulfill his promise.

The informant's use of the Spanish phrase "*no cumplió la promesa*" implies a stronger sense of commitment than the English word "promise," for it is the same phrase used in describing the fulfillment of a religious vow.

Obregón represented in many ways the new class of people emerging in the Mayo region and in other parts of the country. This was the merchant class, successors to the group that originally made up the Alamos-based support for Ignacio Pesqueira in the 19th century. In other parts of Mexico, groups with interests similar to those of the Alameños were also ready to join the revolutionary cause against the ruling class. Chafing under the gerontocracy of Díaz, and dissatisfied with his attempts to develop their economically depressed country, the leaders of the Revolution convinced the peasants and the workers that they had common interests. In a sense they were correct, and history has to some extent vindicated them, for the Revolution created profound social and economic changes without which Mexico could never have reached the level of development it now enjoys. The greater part of that enjoyment, however, is experienced by the bourgeoisie that began and led the Revolution (Beene 1972:5, 143).

Obregón was committed to a progress disdained by the prerevolutionary ruling class. It was through his efforts and the efforts of his successors that the Mayo valley was transformed from a tribal homeland into one of the most productive and technologically advanced agricultural regions of Mexico. That this change was wrought at the expense of the Mayos caused little consternation among Mestizos. The irony is that without the support of Mayo and Yaqui troops it is doubtful that Obregón could have achieved the military successes that made possible the Mayos' ultimate disenfranchisement.

The Legacy of the Revolution

In the years following the success of Obregón's military efforts, the economic development of the Mayo region was slow but constant, and the Indians who had fought for autonomy were given land-reform plots instead. The heroes of the Revolution were thus tied irretrievably into the national economy and political organization. Any remaining activism was defused by the granting of minimal landholding units, while the safety of Mestizo development projects was assured. These projects, begun in 1892 and interrupted by the Revolution, were resumed after 1926, when legislation was passed by the new government for the creation of irrigation systems in the Mexican northwest (Dunbier 1968:200). These works were begun in earnest in the early 1930s, but the first goals of government were to improve yields on existing irrigated lands--those in the hands of Mestizos--rather than to open new lands to irrigated agriculture (Dozier 1963:552).

During this period there remained some unrest in southern Sonora, for Yaqui raids were not unknown even in the 1930s. In 1931 and 1935, furthermore, Mestizo residents of the Mayo region raided Mayo churches, burning the wooden statues of the saints and often the churches themselves. The context for these actions was the anti-clerical campaign being waged throughout the state by Governor Rodolfo Elías Calles. However, it is probable that the Mestizos saw in the burning of the saints an opportunity to retaliate for former Mayo actions. Mayos still refer to the burning of the saints as defining an era, and point to it as one of the low points in the history of the Mayo region.

The passivity of the Indians at this outrage against their way of life is an indicator that they were indeed pacified. Although they carried off statues of saints and hid them, they did not offer active resistance to the Mestizo attackers. This type of passive resistance to Mestizo inroads seems to have characterized inter-ethnic relations ever since the Revolution: while as late as 1905 canal-builders required armed guards to protect them from Indian raids (Troncoso 1905:203), development was relatively unimpeded after the 1926 irrigation laws were passed and began to be implemented. It is still impossible, however, to find Mayos willing to work in the fields during the various fiesta periods, much to the consternation of the Mestizo landowners.

In 1936, Román Yocupicio was elected Governor of Sonora. A native of the Mayo valley and himself Mayo, Yocupicio had served as a general under Obregón. Proclaiming his solidarity with the Indians, Yocupicio attained by "diplomacy" what decades of fighting had failed to achieve. Appealing to the Mayos to consider the needs of their fellow-countrymen, Yocupicio personally negotiated the distribution of the last of the Mayo lands to Mayos and Mestizos alike. In the three municipios in the lower Mayo valley, more than 42,000 hectares of land were distributed in 1938 alone (Garibldi 1939:177-178, 186), although much of this land was not irrigated at that time (Medina 1941:134). Migrants began pouring into the Mayo valley to take advantage of the new land; the population of the valley grew from 62,500 in 1940 to 85,000 in 1950 (ibid., p.57; Sonora, Estado de, 1957:cuadro 2A), largely as a result of migration.

With the distribution of Mayo tribal lands by the government, the stage was set for the dramatic economic development of the Mayo valley in the 1950s. When control over the land passed definitively into the hands of the government, it could plan an effective irrigation system for the region. In 1955 the Mocúzari dam on the Mayo river was completed, providing irrigation for 30,000 hectares of new land (Dozier 1963:549, 553). The Nogales-Guadalajara highway, finished in 1953, made possible more effective transportation of crops and consumer goods. Rural electrification programs were implemented, and one of the first regions to benefit was the Mayo valley (Sonora, Estado de, 1957:263). Migration continued, and the population of the lower Mayo soared from 85,000 in 1950 to close to 120,000 in 1960 (Erasmus 1961:190, 192).

If migrants were lured to Sonora by stories of new lands, many must have been disappointed by the slowing of the land reform begun by Yocupicio. The large amount of land distributed by his administration increased government land-grant farms from 13% to 40% of all farmland in the state, thus benefiting the landless if coincidentally finally disenfranchising the Mayos. However, between 1940 and 1950 land-grant farms dropped to 17% of all farm land. This change was due to the sharp increase in private holdings, most often large farms. In the 1930s, under the administration of President Lázaro Cárdenas, large holdings were broken up and land reform was of major interest to the government. The administrations that followed Cárdenas' were less concerned with land reform than with industrial development, and this is demonstrated by the increase in large landholdings in Sonora in the 1950s (Alcantara 1976:144-180).

The result of this change in land policy was that many migrants, as well as native Mayos, who had hoped to become farmers became farmworkers instead. The technologically oriented bourgeoisie that had led the Revolution now became the new ruling elite of Sonora. Large farmers married into commercial families, thus insuring the continued stability of both elements of the economy. The national government, eager to promote self-sufficiency in food production, and intimidated by threats of agricultural strikes, was easily convinced of the wisdom of allowing large enterprises to flourish in Sonora, although this policy eventually led to the underutilization of technical inputs and ultimately to recession (ibid., p. 165).

The spectacular development in southern Sonora in the 1950s, then, benefited those who were least in need of help. In the meantime the Mayos, integrated perforce into the national system, were effectively marginalized within it. They had gained a modicum of prosperity, in terms of material goods and social opportunities, but at the cost of their political and economic autonomy.

Conclusion

By 1960, the Mayo valley had been almost completely transformed: where once the thorn forest was interrupted only by Mayo subsistence plots, vast expanses of commercial crops now grew. The land so tenaciously held and fought over for centuries was divided into land-grant and private plots which, if not entirely in the possession of Mestizos, were governed by Mestizo laws and Mestizo leaders. The autonomy that Mayos had begun to lose in the 19th century was now only a memory. The modern world, in the form of mechanized agriculture and consumer goods, had come to stay. The Mayos, however, participated only marginally in the progress that had overwhelmed their homeland. Living as small farmers and farmworkers, they had only limited access to the benefits of civilization. While their standard of living undoubtedly rose, they continued to participate in their ancient ceremonies and to live in many ways as they always had. Those who found opportunities to become wealthy in the new system lost their Mayo identity and joined the Mestizo ranks, but the majority of Mayos were less affected by the events of the 1950s than were the newcomers to the region. To understand why this occurred, it is necessary to examine precisely what is meant by development, its effects, and how and why these effects differ.

2

Theoretical Perspectives on Economic Development and Ethnic Identity

Theories of Economic Development and Ethnic Identity

The theoretical issue central to this study is the relationship between economic development and ethnic identity, not only in the Mayo area but in general. The concepts of economic development and plural society both derive from the European colonial experience, but with few exceptions (e.g. Geertz 1963a, 1963b; Nagata 1979), little attempt has been made to understand specifically the relationship between the two. The existing literature cannot be ignored, however, for several reasons. In the first place, theories on the causes and consequences of economic growth have been the basis of development programs throughout the world; as such, they have had a great impact on the subsequent effects of such programs not only on national economies but on individual lives. The theoretical assumptions about human interaction upon which these programs were based had much to do with these effects. Theories on plural societies and ethnic minorities have rarely had such real-world consequences as the economic theories, but do provide a way of examining ethnic identity and its role in social dynamics. A third group of studies, focusing on the use of religious symbols to express social realities, is also relevant to the question at hand.

In all these works, the core concern is the relationship between cultural symbols and social relations. How this relationship is seen colors every aspect of the theories presented. Taken together, these three bodies of literature point the way toward a theoretical perspective that embraces both the social and cultural circumstances in the Mayo valley.

In the literature on development, and in much of that on ethnic identity, there is an assumption that aspects of society such as economic and political structures determine such cultural elements as language use, religion, and ethnic identity. It is thought that if change occurs in the economic structure, commensurate cultural changes will follow. The alternate view is that cultural traits are primordial, immutable aspects of human perception that, once learned, can be changed only with great difficulty; this assumption is found more commonly in works on ethnic identity and on symbolism (Shils 1957; Geertz 1963a, 1963b; Turner 1974). To the extent that this latter supposition exists in the development literature, the cultural traits of "traditional" societies are seen as blocking or slowing the pace of economic and political development (McClelland 1963; Foster 1965; Geertz 1963a).

The theory that changes in the economy would bring about general cultural modernization inspired most of the development programs first implemented after World War II. It was further assumed that economic growth could occur only in the context of a certain amount of social inequality. The goal in agriculture was to increase overall production by developing special strains of seeds and introducing technology developed in the industrialized nations. Mechanization of agriculture, which is more efficient on large parcels, overshadowed the desires of rural people for land reform (Erasmus 1974). It was hoped that mechanization would eventually free the predominantly rural populations of developing nations for work in industry. In the rush to promote overall growth, there was little concern over which segments of the population benefited from these policies; indeed, the encouragement of efficiency and entrepreneurship automatically biased programs in favor of the relatively wealthy. Development agencies were aware of the problem of inequality (Morawetz 1977:8), but they assumed that the poor would eventually be better off than they had been, although absolute equality could not be hoped for.

This "trickle-down" theory dominated much of the thinking on economic development through the 1960s. It implied in many ways a commitment to the free-enterprise system in which capitalist development first occurred, and a hope that by tinkering with the system it might be made to work in a world no longer pristine in terms of capitalism.

The results of the first development programs, and the effects of their shortcomings, are complex. It must be pointed out that in most cases economic growth did occur (Morawetz 1977:12-19). However, this growth was accompanied by disturbances unforeseen by the development agencies. The trickle-down theory's application caused the emergence of entrenched elites unwilling to part with their new wealth and endowed with the power to keep it. In the agricultural areas, the "green revolution," along with land reform, did make some countries independent in food production, but even these programs tended to benefit those already well off; the political structures of most Third World countries and the prevailing lack of education made it unlikely that the very poorest would receive land or technical aid (Andrews 1963; de Alcantara 1976; Adelman and Morris 1973).

In reaction to the unequal benefits of the trickle-down theory, new proposals for Third World nations began to emerge in the 1960s. Frank (1973) pointed out that their underdevelopment was historically tied to the development of the former imperial nations: the latter needed the raw materials of the colonies in order to industrialize, and the colonies provided markets for industrial goods. Frank accused development agencies of perpetuating this dependency rather than eliminating it. Meanwhile Stavenhagen (1965), González-Casanova (1965) and other Latin American scholars focused on the uneven distribution of wealth within their nations. They advocated the redistribution of income and the implementation of programs designed to promote growth of the poorest sectors of the economy. To these writers, the trickle-down theory seemed ineffective in promoting the kind of growth needed to create a truly good society. On the contrary, development programs seemed to be creating societies with permanently marginalized groups which would never benefit from the economic changes happening before their eyes.

Wallerstein's (1976) concept of the modern world-system, based on exhaustive historical research, explains why particular development programs, and indeed the whole approach to Third World development, do not work. This is because the core nations, former colonial empires, continue their economic relationship with the former colonies, the periphery of the world-system. The core nations control capital and technology, and extract low-value raw materials in exchange for these high-cost inputs. Therefore, the development projects, which feature foreign investment, foreign loans, and technology transfer, actually increase the economic dependence of Third World nations on the developed nations. The international debt situation of the 1980s is a classic example of this dependence and its ultimate effects on the economies of the periphery nations.

Within these nations the global situation can be found in miniature (Germani 1980:5). The economic and political elites control capital and technology, often using them to become even wealthier, while the poorest are left out, except to be used as cheap labor. Lack of education, skills, and other opportunities means that those most in need of help become marginalized.

Marginality, broadly conceived, is the exclusion of people from participation in the national economy and political system. In the economic sphere, this exclusion may be on the production or the consumption side, or both. Politically, lack of access to decision-making at the national as well as the local level can be factors of marginality (Germani 1980:3-6). Essentially, the marginalized are cut off from the kinds of opportunities development programs are supposed to offer in order to bring about modernization: education, a living wage, and political power for the majority of the population. The exclusion of the poorest from these opportunities can create a permanent underclass that, undereducated and without economic resources, is a perennial drag on true growth.

It is well to note the practical outcome of the theoretical assumptions motivating early development programs such as the one in the Mayo valley. The view that culture is mostly, if not entirely, governed by social-structural variables underlay most of these programs. However, by simply making changes in economic and political organization, these programs created something of a monster: not only did the people most in need of aid not receive it, but the cultural diversity that emerged in response to social changes is too diverse to be given any one name such as "modern" or "traditional."

Benedict (1962) stresses the importance of the economic structure of a society over the ethnic groups or cultures that comprise it. He describes the change in the ethnic make-up of classes in Mauritius, and asserts that this is due not to changes in the cultural elements of the ethnic groups but to alterations in the political and economic structure of the society. Because these are the determinants of how plural a society is in terms of culture traits, Benedict (p.1244) finds pluralism to be nothing more than a descriptive category: "Where political and economic conditions permit, pluralism tends to break down. . . . Where political and economic opportunities are distributed on the basis of ascribed ethnic or cultural status, divisive tendencies develop."

The Mayo case demonstrates the rather simplistic nature of this formulation. Individuals and families at the Mayo extreme of the cultural continuum are in general less well off than their more Mestizo neighbors; however, in the Mayo region opportunities are not distributed on the basis of ascribed ethnic or cultural status. On the other hand, the Mayo language and religious traditions persist, upheld by individuals who clearly display some interest in maintaining them. The social system in the Mayo valley, then, lies somewhere between Benedict's two categories. In fact, this is a case that is too complex to be accommodated by Benedict's theory.

Benedict's view echoes the Weberian idea (Weber 1970) implicit in many development programs: as a society becomes more rational and less traditional, the ascribed statuses are replaced by achieved statuses-- meritocracy replaces oligarchy. This position, which defines culture traits as dependent upon social structure, predicts that as economic opportunities allow for social mobility, class identity becomes more important than ethnicity in determining behavior. This so-called "melting-pot" theory would have Furnivall's (1948) medley combine rather than merely mix. The axiom that society determines culture has as its corollary that when two cultures come into contact, they will in fact combine into one with traits from both, given an open social structure (Gordon 1964:114-131; Shibutani and Kwan 1965:118-120; Barth 1969).

In Mexico, this view of acculturation was espoused by the founders of the Instituto Nacional Indigenista (INI). The INI policy, developed in opposition to the Social Darwinism of the Porfiriato, has consistently been to provide economic opportunities for Indians in the hope that they will eventually be assimilated into the national society. The amount of governmental concern for the Indians in monetary terms has always been much smaller than the output for straight economic growth such as is seen in the Mayo valley, but to the extent that this concern has been expressed it has had as its goal the merging of the Indians into the national culture. This policy has provided the basis for all of the INI's development programs, including those in Sonora.

Theoretical Perspectives

A somewhat different focus on ethnic identity and complex societies began to develop during the 1960s. Responding to the clear re-emergence of ethnic consciousness in the United States and to the continuing problems of ethnic groups in Third World countries, social scientists coined the term "ethnic minorities." This refers to groups that owe their continuity at least in part to systematic structural marginalization processes in the societies where they live. This neo-Marxian view contrasts with the decidedly Weberian focus of most previous work, although the assumption that social structure determines ethnicity remains largely intact. The social structure that places minorities at the bottom of the opportunity ladder is blamed for a vicious circle of marginalization and low expectations from which minority members find it difficult to escape (Lewis 1959). Somewhat more extreme in their position are the dependency theorists (Stavenhagen 1965; González-Casanova 1970; Dow 1973; Barrera et al. 1972; Almaguer 1971; Moore 1970). These authors see the social, economic, and political forces of the dominant segments of complex societies as consciously preventing the equal distribution of essential goods and services; those who are left out by the system are in many cases ethnic minorities. Friedlander (1975:71-75) goes so far as to say that the Indians in a central Mexico village she studied are forced into an identity which they regard as completely negative. This identity, originally imposed by the Spanish, continues to be applied by Mestizo individuals and representatives of modern Mexican social institutions.

In the terminology of these authors, the Mayos are indeed an ethnic minority; their minority status derives in many ways from their economic and political position in the region. However, the extreme diversity of opportunities within the Mayo area makes necessary a closer examination of the relationship between ethnic behavior and social constraints. In fact, there are some social situations, such as Mayo religious events, in which people who are Mestizos in other contexts assert that they are Mayos. The nature of ethnic behavior and ethnic identity in general, while affected by economic and political opportunities or the lack of them, is not entirely determined by them.

The assumption that social structure determines cultural values led to a rather lopsided view of human behavior; little attention was paid to actual culture content, or to the role of symbols in giving meaning to social behavior. Writing concurrently with scholars such as Benedict, other students of ethnic identity have tended to downplay structural factors in favor of the primordiality of ethnic ties. Shils (1957) and Geertz (1963a) have to varying degrees delineated the position that ethnic identity is at least to some extent a result of the circumstances of one's birth, and consequently immutable. These authors believe that the role of ethnic ties in organizing such aspects of social structure as political entities and economic endeavors indicates that cultural variables are the deciding factors in how societies change or do not change. Culture content, ethnic symbols, and affective relationships explain social interaction.

Spicer (1971) attempts to combine the concept of marginality, and the opposition it implies between the marginalized and the dominant culture, with the primordialist idea of immutable cultural symbols. The term "enclave" is used to describe cultural systems that owe their continuity to this combination of structural opposition and internal cultural cohesion. This model has been used successfully by Keyes (1979) and others (Castile and Kushner 1981) to explain cultural persistence in the absence of such structures as territory and language. However, its usefulness is somewhat limited to cultures demonstrating persistence rather than change. It does take into account both social-structural and cultural aspects of ethnicity, but it does not explain ethnic change or social dynamics within and between ethnic categories. Enclaves are seen as being equally unchanging and immutable as the peoples studied by the primordialists.

The idea that primordial cultural phenomena such as membership in ethnic groups take precedence over social change goes against the optimism of development programs and of the melting-pot model of ethnic assimilation: if cultural elements, learned from birth, cannot be changed, how can we progress? This is a rather extreme expression of what is actually a wide spectrum of views on primordial ties; however, it points up the difficulty of the primordialist position with respect to economic development: rapid social change can only be defeated by traditional allegiances; worse yet, economic development programs may destroy the delicate balance of traditional cultures and lead to cultural disintegration.

Such a dark view of the potential of human society is probably unwarranted; nevertheless, the role of cultural symbols in maintaining social life, however traditional or progressive, is certainly more important than is assumed by many melting-pot theorists. In line with his earlier work on primordial entities, and in reaction to the aridity of structurally oriented studies, Geertz in 1966 called for a return to the study of religious symbols and their role in defining and interpreting social reality. In the same volume (Banton 1966), Turner demonstrates the usefulness of culturally established categories of perception in dealing with social conflicts.

Similar themes have continued to concern both of these authors in the intervening years. Turner points out in several works (1967; 1974) that symbols are multivocal--that is, they mean different things to different people and in different situations. This ambiguity of symbolic meaning makes symbols useful in expressing and mending rents in the fabric of social relations. Through ritual, social structure is expressed and reinforced.

Turner has rarely looked to ethnic matters for inspiration, although the African culture he studied was within a plural society. Likewise, Geertz' interests have with few exceptions (1963a, 1963b) skirted ethnicity as a system of cultural symbols. However, Geertz (1971) does demonstrate how ambiguous religious symbols are manipulated in the context of cultural diversity. Comparing varieties of Islamic belief and ritual in two societies, themselves diverse culturally, he shows how symbols serve both to unite different social segments into a symbolic whole and at the same time to reinforce the diversity itself. Geertz goes beyond Turner here in considering the role of symbols and rituals in the process of social change and political development.

Geertz' study of Islam is especially useful in the study of world religions as complex cultural systems. The symbols of Islam are ambiguous enough to be accepted by a wide variety of societies. Catholicism, similarly, provides a rich and various complex of beliefs and rituals that are sufficiently multivocalic to allow for immensely diverse interpretation by the societies that accept them. In the Mayo region there exist, sometimes simultaneously, three distinct versions of Catholic belief and ritual: the orthodox system overseen by the priests, the folk system, and a Mayo revitalization movement. All claim to be Catholic, and all share enough to accept the validity of each other's versions; however, the three systems show little sign of merging. This is because each system serves to express, validate, and sometimes change the social realities of the people who participate in the rituals. In many respects, though not all, the kind of religious rituals an individual participates in indicate ethnic identity.

Saussure's (1966) discussion of the difference between *langue* and *parole* is of interest in the discussion of religion and ethnic identity. "Langue" is seen as the underlying rules of a language, and "parole" consists of the actual use of these rules in everyday speech. Writers such as Lévi-Strauss (1963) and others (Sahlins 1981; Goodenough 1956) have used this distinction in analyzing cultural behavior; their intention is to derive the underlying rules from observed behavior. My own desire is to explain observed behavior as a manipulation of the rules--symbols, in the present context--in order to establish, maintain, or change the individual's role in the social order. That the rules are ambiguous and subject to a variety of interpretations merely indicates the complexity of the human mind and its consequent ability to create complex social orders based on a few organizing concepts. Language, the most purely symbolic of human behaviors, is also the key to understanding the rest of them. Symbols of ethnic identity, like ritual symbols, have meaning because of the structures in people's minds. However, the extent to which these symbols are used, displayed, or concealed is influenced by ongoing economic and political exchanges, as well as by specific social situations.

We can perhaps best see the relationship between culture and society as a dialectic: neither is the independent variable; rather, each determines the other according to the historical realities of a given society. The nature of individual behavior derives, then, from a complex interplay between symbols and social relations: the individual manipulates symbols according to elaborate rules of action based on rewards and punishments experienced in social interaction. The existence of symbols depends on the endurance of social relations as much as these depend on symbols for all human endeavors.

It is necessary to examine both cultural and social variables in any attempt to understand the nature of ethnic identity in complex societies. Ethnic minorities often exist because of a lack of opportunities in the dominant segments of these societies; however, it is naive to insist that this marginalization alone is responsible for the continued existence of ethnic entities. It is equally simplistic to assume that ethnic identity is immutable, programmed by symbolic means from infancy and not responsive to external social situations. Rather, the relationship between culture traits--in this case the meaning of ethnic symbols--and social structure is dynamic, complex, and subject to situational and historical changes.

People at the Mayo extreme of the cultural continuum, for example, have on the whole been marginalized economically and politically with respect to much of the remaining population. However, the specific manifestations of this general marginalization vary from community to community and from family to family. The responses to this great variety in the pattern of marginalization feature manipulations of ethnic symbols such as language and ritual. The way these symbols are used and the meaning attributed to them vary with the historical, ecological, and economic factors affecting each community and each individual. Ethnic symbols also come into play differently in different social situations; in all cases, individuals seek their own best interest in exhibiting explicitly ethnic behavior or in downplaying ethnicity. At the same time, the ongoing use of ethnic symbols helps to define, interpret, and sometimes change the nature of social relations. In the context of tremendous social changes brought about by development, cultural symbols provide the multivocality--the variety of possible interpretations--needed to emcompass the complexity of social relations.

Economic Development in the Mayo Region

Weber's idea that rationalization of the social structure would bring about a general cultural modernization was the basis for Mexico's economic development programs, which were enormously successful in terms of overall growth. During the years 1940 to 1970, Mexico experienced some of the most spectacular economic growth ever recorded. Agricultural production increased by an average of 8.2% annually between 1940 and 1950. Agriculture also became more efficient: between 1940 and 1962, the average per capita production grew by 68% (Hansen 1971:41). This increase was largely due to government-financed inputs such as land reform, technical aid, and credit assistance, as well as the mammoth irrigation projects in Sonora and Sinaloa. However, by 1970 a certain strain began to show in the Mexican economy. Agricultural production leveled off, and no new irrigation projects such as the Sonoran marvels were in the works. In addition, the population growth rate had almost equaled the rate of economic growth, thus eradicating the potential benefits of development (Wellhausen 1976). Furthermore, the distribution of these benefits was less edifying than were the production

Theoretical Perspectives

statistics. Adelman and Morris (1973:152), in their analysis of a large number of development variables, discovered that Mexico's economy was one of the least distributive in the world.

These kinds of statistics led to the call for more redistributive development programs, but for Mexico it was already too late. President Luis Echeverría (1970-76) attempted to institute such policies. Government spending in agriculture increased 700% during his administration, and most of the increase was directed toward small farmers. He also instituted an aggressive land-reform program. Unfortunately, these policies succeeded only in creating an unbearable rate of inflation, bankrupting the national economy, and ultimately alienating rich and poor alike.

In the years since the Echeverría debacle, Mexico's economy has been on something of a seesaw. The discovery of oil in the southeastern section of the country in 1976 was expected to solve the economic problems created by Echeverría. There was indeed a small boom brought on by oil production between 1978 and 1981 (World Bank 1986:35), when the national economy grew at a rate of 8% per year. The drop in oil prices which began in 1981, the ensuing international debt crisis, and the regular devaluation of the peso against the U.S. dollar have created an economic downturn that has affected the entire nation. In Sonora, for example, daily wages for agricultural workers rose from 100 pesos in 1977 to 3,000 pesos in 1987, but the dollar value of this pay fell from $5 U.S. to $3 in that period. In the country as a whole, interest rates for agricultural credit rose from 15% in 1977 to 85% in 1987.

Other data point to the general downward direction of Mexico's economy after 1970. The agricultural production growth rate fell from 5.4% for the period 1965 to 1973 to 3.4% for 1973-1984. Agricultural imports totaled 2.9 million metric tons in 1974; this rose to 8.5 million in 1984. Meanwhile, population growth averaged 2.9% per annum in the 1973-1984 period, while government expenditure decreased by 8.5% of the gross national product (World Bank 1986:183-229). All of these statistics have translated into a reduction of new economic and social opportunities for Mexicans, which has resulted in a dramatic increase in emigration to the United States.

The pattern of development in Mexico as a nation is echoed in the Mayo valley: all the drama of spectacular growth and all the tragedy of stagnation can be found there. Most of Mexico's rural development occurred in Sonora and Sinaloa, and much of the subsequent backlash also. Irrigation projects were begun as early as the turn of the century in the Mayo valley. These and later works were constructed privately and were designed to increase productivity on lands already cleared and firmly in the hands of Mestizos who had encroached on Mayo tribal territory. This territory was irrevocably broken up during the administration of Lázaro Cárdenas (1935-40), who is famous for his far-reaching land-reform program. In the nation as a whole, this program divided the lands of the wealthy and gave them to the poor in the form of ejidos. In the Mayo region, the ejido lands consisted mainly of Mayo tribal lands, although some haciendas also were expropriated.

Thus the Mayos were confronted with the ultimate irony of the Revolution: they fought to keep their land, and then received it in the form of patronage from the government they had helped bring to power. Their status as a formerly autonomous entity was ignored; land was distributed to those who had petitioned for it, regardless of ethnic identity. Unwittingly, the Mayos more than many other Indian groups in Mexico helped bring about Cárdenas' goal of creating a nation of peasants and workers securely tied into the political system that he headed. Today, the Sonoran peasantry are so completely tied to the national government that their economic survival depends almost entirely upon it.

Beyond fulfilling the political goals of the new elite, land reform in the Mayo valley also defused a potentially explosive situation. By helping to provide the poor of the nation with a subsistence, it made them conservative and unwilling to risk their meager plots for the sake of greater autonomy. By creating ejidos composed of both Mayos and Mestizo newcomers to the region, the land-reform program also began to dissipate ethnic solidarity among the Mayos, who had fought so long for cultural and political autonomy.

In the meantime, vast tracts of uncleared land were made available to private buyers (Alcantara 1976:145). It was these private farmers who, with the aid of government-supported irrigation works and protective tariffs, brought about Mexico's agricultural miracle: 90% of the increase in wheat production in northwest Mexico was on private holdings larger than 5 hectares. In Sonora, the increase in wheat production on private holdings represented 56% of the increase in all of northern Mexico between 1940 and 1960 (Hansen 1971:396). The private farmers on whose land these increases took place constitute today an entrenched agricultural elite whose political control of all of southern Sonora was demonstrated when this group successfully resisted Echeverría's land-reform program in 1975 and 1976 (Sanderson 1981:3-5). This colossally uneven distribution of wealth and power is a direct legacy of the development program. It also expresses the realization of the dreams of Obregón and his Sonoran allies.

While private farmers were producing immense quantities of wheat and cotton, the descendants of Totoliguoqui were not faring quite so well. Ejidatarios struggled to keep their parcels and feed their families. Ejido organizations were weak, and the government bank was corrupt. Many ejido members, unable to get credit and ill-prepared to practice the kind of mechanized farming expected by the government, illegally rented all or part of their land to private farmers. The plight of landless farm workers was even worse than that of ejidatarios. The population explosion of the early development years created more people than could be accommodated by new ejidos, and wage laborers suffered in two ways in Sonora. In the first place, mechanization on large farms diminished the need for unskilled labor. Second, real wages decreased during this period of Mexico's greatest economic growth (Alcantara 1976:132). The very poorest of Sonora's poor became more impoverished, while the rich flourished under government protection.

Here, apparently, is a classic example of the kind of development deplored by those favoring redistributive strategies: overall growth occurred, but at the expense of the original residents, who now compose a marginalized underclass exploited by the wealthy or by government agents. However, it would be unfair to insist that the poor, mostly Mayos, were excluded entirely from the benefits of Sonoran development. Apart from the obviously greater share in public funding for irrigation, Sonora also has consistently had more electrical plants, more roads and more government-sponsored medical facilities per capita than its population justifies (O'Connor 1980:70). This generally high standard of living in itself accrued more to the wealthy than to the poor, but even the poorest in Sonora live better today as a result of development.

The general rise in the standard of living in Sonora obscures the great diversity in the consequences of development even in such a small area as the Mayo valley. Here, these consequences were diverse from the beginning, and have changed over time. In the first place, the coming of irrigation and large amounts of government expenditure in the 1950s led to an economic boom that made some farmers millionaires overnight. At a level far below this, a small middle class of merchants, farmers, and bureaucrats emerged. This group engaged in classic Veblenian competitive consumption, adding to economic and social progress by buying modern consumer goods such as refrigerators and televisions (Erasmus 1961). Because the soaring growth rates of the 1940s, '50s and '60s subsided after 1970, this class is no longer the burgeoning phenomenon it was in 1958; nevertheless, it still represents a social status to which even the poor can aspire. This group, then, fills the enormous gap between rich and poor, thereby reducing somewhat the relative deprivation experienced by many. Still, before the coming of development there was little opportunity for relative deprivation in the Mayo valley--all were Mayos and all were poor, by modern standards.

The emergence of a middle class in the towns and cities of the Mayo region was only one of the many consequences of the development program, and an early one at that. Indeed, the great cultural variety found in the Mayo valley in 1987 would seem to belie the fact that the region's economy depends entirely on agriculture. This diversity is the direct result of an uneven distribution of economic and social opportunities in the region as a whole. The kinds of opportunities made available either directly or indirectly by government assistance vary according to ecological and historical circumstances. For example, people living in areas already densely populated at the time of the land reform were less likely to receive land from the government, simply because there was not enough to distribute. People who lived outside the irrigation district were even worse off, for land without water is relatively useless in this arid environment. Finally, there were those fortunate areas where sparse population and available water combined to make possible efficient mechanized farming of the sort envisioned by the planners of the development program. Most of the land in these areas, of course, went to private farmers who then prospered tremendously. There are, however, some ejidos in these areas, and the economic and social opportunities here are far greater than elsewhere.

It is not enough to document a variety of government-induced opportunities, for individual access to these opportunities also varies even within the same ecological subregion. In some cases, sheer luck--being in the right place at the right time--has been a significant factor in the success of individual families. Ability to perceive and make use of available opportunities is also important. Thus, the person who is familiar with the ways of government agencies, who has many social and political networks and who knows how to use these, will prosper more than someone who is ill-at-ease outside his own family and kin group. The ability to speak fluent Spanish rather than the easily identifiable Spanish of the native Mayo-speaker is a bonus. Similarly, communities that for a variety of reasons are cohesive enough to agree on common goals and on how to achieve them are more successful than the community racked by internal dissension, regardless of the existence of opportunities or lack of them.

It is the interplay between the diverse opportunities of the region and the behavior of individuals and communities who use them that generates the bewildering variety of economic, social, and ethnic circumstances to be found in the Mayo valley. To be sure, the development program is responsible for creating the diversity of opportunities, and many who would otherwise have been poor are rich because they know how to manipulate situations that exist only as a result of development. Beyond this, it is impossible to state categorically whether or not the program has been a "success," precisely because definitions of success differ widely and the effects themselves are so diverse.

Given this diversity, it would be possible for both the melting-pot theory and the dependency theory to be substantiated in the Mayo valley. There are segments of the population easily described as a marginalized ethnic enclave (N. Ross Crumrine 1981); conversely, there are whole families once considered Mayo who now see themselves as de razón, or Mestizo. However, there are also individuals and families outside of both these groups, occupying a great variety of ethnic niches. Finally, some people's ethnic status is still in the process of change. When economic diversity is combined with this ethnic diversity, it becomes clear that we must go beyond existing theories in order to explain the social situation in the Mayo region.

Theoretical Perspectives

Ethnic Identity in the Mayo Valley

If economic and political structures provide the context for social relations, it is through the manipulation of cultural symbols that meaning is given to these relations in everyday life. To the extent that social relations are made complex by economic and political structures, cultural symbols will be similarly multivocalic. In the Mayo valley, whether or not specifically ethnic symbols are used depends upon a complex interaction of historical, ecological, and economic factors. Before the economic development program, both the structure of the plural society and the content of the ethnic symbols were fairly simple. The hacendados and merchants in the area were wealthy, and their cultural ties were with others of their economic station throughout Sonora, but especially in the city of Alamos. There was little chance of confusing these people with the indigenous inhabitants of the area, who had an established traditional culture and few ties beyond the Mayo region. The medley observed by Furnivall (1948) was also found in the Mayo valley: when Mayos and Mestizos interacted, it was only in the context of economic and political exchanges; the cultures did not combine.

Development, of course, brought many changes in the economic and political structures of the area. These changes were so numerous and so far-reaching that no one could have foreseen them in devising the development plan. The cultural means that the people themselves elaborated to give meaning to these changes are equally complex. Because there existed two separate cultures in the valley, some of the cultural symbols have necessarily taken on ethnic values, for ethnicity can be a powerful tool for expressing social distinctions. However, because of the relative fluidity of the new social structure and the blurring of precise ethnic symbols, the mask of ethnic identity can be donned, doffed, or changed with relative ease. In turn, the ease of ethnic change is to a large extent limited by economic and political factors.

In general, the nature of social relations has been made more complex, rather than simpler, as predicted by the melting-pot theory. The cultural symbols used to express this diversity are similarly complex and have different meanings in different situations. Individuals with the greatest knowledge of symbols and their various meanings in different contexts have the greatest success socially and economically. Those who are most fully bilingual in Mayo and Spanish have access to the broadest range of cultural expression in this context. Likewise, communities with the greatest flexibility in using a variety of cultural symbols will have the greatest success in obtaining economic and political favors from the government. However, historical and ecological factors, as well as the vagaries of development itself, impose limits on how much specific individuals and communities participate in the complex social structure of the region.

Development, then, brought about a sort of social explosion in the Mayo valley: existing social structures were disrupted, new economic and political structures were introduced, and others came about in response to the program itself. The resulting social milieu has for the most part crystallized since 1970, the year in which new opportunities began to be less abundant. The development explosion provided a host of new opportunities, but not everyone had access to these opportunities. Those individuals with the greatest knowledge and power gained the most from development; those with the least actually suffered. If development could be eternal, the trickle-down theory might work, eventually. The actual outcome in the Mayo valley is a continuum of economic opportunities from those affording immense wealth to those imposing extreme poverty. The resulting cultural continuum provides the symbols by which individuals affirm, mask, or try to change their status within the system. Whether or not these symbols are intended and perceived as ethnic is determined by specific social situations.

One way to discuss the social and cultural continuum is to define the extremes: the people with the most social opportunities and consequently the most cosmopolitan, "modern" Mexican national culture are at one end of this continuum. Those with the fewest social and economic opportunities make up the most "traditional" Mayo culture at the other end. In structural terms, these two are vestiges of the pre-development plural society; people at the extremes rarely interact, and never in any but contexts involving economic exchanges. Today, the extremes form only a minority of the population of the area. Between the two extremes is a social and cultural continuum whose variety is only partially explored in this work.

The terms used to define ethnic categories are also vestiges of the pre-development social structure. These terms include those used by individuals to describe themselves and each other; in addition, terms used throughout Latin America are also recognized within this conceptual framework. For example, the term "de razón" is used to define a non-Indian; most often this is used by those who so identify themselves. This corresponds to what many anthropologists (N. Ross Crumrine 1968; Friedlander 1975) call "Mestizo;" in general it implies a certain amount of similarity or affinity with the Mexican national culture, itself heavily influenced by U.S. culture today. Those who do not see themselves as members of this category use the term "yori" to describe it. This is a somewhat pejorative term, but the extent to which it is seen as derogatory depends extensively on situational factors. "Mayo" is used, like Mestizo, in a rather nonjudgmental way in the anthropological literature; like Mestizo, it is rarely used by anyone in the Mayo valley, except in reference to the geographical region itself. People who wish to contrast themselves to yoris call themselves "yoreme;" those who call themselves "de razón" call others "indios".

These conceptual categories were used before the development program was begun, but they have been pressed into service to define a social reality that has become more complex as a result of development. For example, the same individual may be considered a yori by others and yet claim yoreme status based on one or more of several criteria. Furthermore, there is a certain amount of overlapping of terms: people will sometimes call themselves yoris, and indio is also used as a self-describing term. The possibly derogatory aspect of these terms is downplayed, although implicit, in certain contexts. An example of this is the individual mentioned earlier who, when asked his ethnic identity, responded that he was "more yoreme than de razón."

At one end of this continuum are the people who benefited most from development. This group includes old Alamos families, but also many people from other parts of Mexico and a few formerly poor Sonorans who happened to be in the right place at the right time in the development process. These are truly millionaires who live in palatial mansions in Huatabampo and Navojoa, the two market towns in the valley. The wives and daughters of these families shop for clothes regularly in the United States, and the sons are educated abroad. These families maintain homes in Mexico City and some have homes in the United States. They aspire to much of the upper-class lifestyle of the United States, but also pay at least lip service to the ideal of the old Sonoran upper class: ownership of cattle, good horsemanship and ability at hunting are valued, as well as such American consumer goods as air-conditioned cars and pickup trucks.

At the other end of the continuum are the unmistakable descendants of Totoliguoqui. These are found in remote hamlets with no electricity or running water. Here, the traditions followed come close to the culture established by the interaction between the Mayos and the Jesuits. Mayo is spoken more than Spanish; adults are nonliterate; clay water-jugs sit on three-pronged stands cut from the natural vegetation. Wattle-and-daub houses and *ramadas*[1] are the customary dwellings, and open-air hearths define the kitchens. Residents of these communities look forward to the Mayo religious fiestas as the high points in an otherwise uninterrupted round of planting (often on the land of the wealthy), irrigating, and harvesting. For them, the fiestas are the main means of interacting socially with people outside the community.

In deference to the primordialists, it must be conceded that for people at both extremes of this continuum ethnic identity is fairly well set and not subject to manipulation. Even if a wealthy Huatabampense wanted to, he could never convince anyone that he was Mayo; likewise, there is no way a rural, Mayo-speaking individual wearing huaraches could pass for a person who is de razón.

If these extremes formed the majority of the population in the valley, the question of ethnicity could be reduced essentially to one of class: the wealthy are de razón, the poor are yoremes. However, the bulk of the population is in the gulf between these two extremes. It is here that, while the circumstances of one's birth are important in determining one's general

---

1. A ramada is a building without walls, affording both shade and fresh air.

place on the cultural continuum, social situations are also instrumental in determining one's behavior. Whether or not this behavior is intended or perceived as ethnic is also dependent on changing situations.

Given the fluidity of the social structure in the area, it is not surprising that the cultural symbols used to define social relations are appropriately ambiguous. For example, it is impossible to obtain a strict definition of the difference between Mayos and Mestizos from the following interviews:

q: It is only the last names that distinguish yoris from yoremes?

a: Yes, only that. Or that the yori doesn't understand the Mayo dialect, that's a yori, even those who live here in the comunidad.

q: But if I learn la lengua (Mayo), will I be a yoreme?

a: No, yori. You can't be a yoreme (laughs).

   (interview with a member of a comunidad indígena)

q: Are there ways of distinguishing between yoris and yoremes here in this hamlet (ranchería)?

a (1): We are all yoremes.

a (2): Here there are no distinctions of work, here yoris are recognized by their color.

a (1): Or because they are from outside, and the yoremes are all natives of this ranchería.

   (interview with residents of a hamlet near Huatabampo)

q: I couldn't become a yoreme?

a: No (laughs). Because how? We are all equal, we all have a soul, often we have the same culture, but being yoreme comes from the customs, because we are alike.

q: What customs do the yoremes have that yoris don't have?

Theoretical Perspectives

a: The part about the vows,[2] which yoris hardly ever make; *velaciones*, *pascolas*, the yoris don't have them. . . .And the way they make their food. The yoris eat food that the yoremes don't know about. For example, the yori eats *picadillo* (hamburger), or asparagus soup. The yoreme eats beans (laughs).

(interview with a resident of Júpare)

This inability to pin down the meaning of ethnic and other cultural symbols indicates their multivocalic quality: the same symbol means different things in different situations. If an individual speaks Mayo in an outlying hamlet, his behavior is not regarded in ethnic terms. Although ethnically neutral, it does serve to continue the norm of speaking Mayo in that social setting. In the town, the same individual speaking Mayo brands himself as an Indian, a country bumpkin suitable for bilking. By the same token, the Spanish-speaker from town is perceived as a stranger worthy of every suspicion if he enters a hamlet where Mayo is normally spoken--he is a yori, someone who may wish harm to country people. Given this ethnic landscape, the hamlet-dweller does his best to speak Spanish without a Mayo accent, and the city resident will bring forward what few words of Mayo he knows to establish rapport. Language, then, is one cultural symbol that is used both to establish or perpetuate social structure and also to express ethnic identity. Like other circumstances of birth in the Mayo area, it can produce different social interpretations in different settings.

Another cultural element often cited by primordialist writers is religion. Religious beliefs and behaviors are more various and more subject to different interpretations than language, however. For example, it is possible to say that the great majority of the residents of the Mayo valley are Catholic. However, the symbols and rituals of the Catholic Church are diverse enough to encompass both the assertion that most are Catholic and the observation that three distinct versions of Catholicism are practiced in the Mayo valley. The distinctions between these versions are easily enough blurred in the appropriate circumstances; likewise, they are clear enough to be the basis of ethnic differentiation should the need for this arise. In addition to these three versions of Catholicism, there are numerous Protestant churches in the region. Depending upon historical factors, participation in one of these religions may or may not be seen as ethnic behavior. In some communities, becoming a Protestant is defined as becoming yori or de razón. In others, no ethnic interpretation is made of conversion, and there are Protestant congregations composed mainly of Mayo-speakers.

---

2. Vows are promises made to God or the saints to perform certain duties. These vows are discussed in Chapter Three.

The apparent paradox of the coexistence of a cultural continuum and ethnic cleavage is perhaps best resolved by the use of a metaphor. It is possible to conceive of ethnicity as two magnetic poles--one Mayo, one Mestizo. In terms of culture traits, individuals fall along a true continuum. In situations ethnically neutral, neither pole is "magnetized," and individuals behave according to their location on the continuum. However, different situations will magnetize one pole or the other, thereby drawing people from all along the continuum to that pole. When this happens, all but those at the very opposite end of the continuum will change their behavior to conform more to that pole. Thus, the Mayo-speaker will speak Spanish and wear shoes in the market town, a Mestizo situation, while he normally speaks Mayo and wears huaraches in his home community. When both poles are magnetized at the same time in the same situation, ethnic conflict may result, because there is a cleavage between the two extremes of allegiance.

As already noted, social situations very often are devoid of ethnic content. Where ethnic cleavages exist, however, behavior that otherwise might be neutral becomes defined as ethnic. In this context, individuals may call on any or all of the criteria for defining ethnicity to substantiate claims for belonging to the ethnic category in question. In situations where Mayo symbols are foremost, people are as Mayo as they can be, bringing forward any symbolic behavior they may know in order to be accepted. The same goes for Mestizo behavior. In some situations, of course, there is ethnic conflict, and individuals must take a stand. It is in these situations only that the cultural continuum breaks in two, so to speak, and the primordial ties of birth take precedence. In the Mayo valley, this type of situation is rare, for there is a general consensus that ethnic conflict should be resolved quickly. To this end, overarching criteria can always be resorted to: when ethnic epithets begin to be hurled, the peacemakers call for a resolution on the basis that "we are all Mexicans," or "we are all Catholics," or even "we are all children of the same God."

The diversity of the social structure and the concomitant fluidity of meaning given to cultural symbols in the Mayo valley make terms like "the Mayo people" meaningless. If one looks only at the people at the Mayo extreme of the continuum, one may find some elements of enclavement (see Crumrine 1981), the consequences of uneven economic development. However, these enclaved people are only a minority of those who see themselves as yoremes. In order to understand and explain ethnicity in this region, the broader context of social relations as a whole must be taken into account.

To return for a moment to Saussure's discussion of langue and parole, we may take ethnic criteria as corresponding to the langue, the rules that give meaning to symbolic behavior. The parole is the subtle manipulation of these rules in everyday life. Just as people use different grammatical constructs and linguistic styles in different social settings, so they may put forth one or more of several kinds of symbolic behavior to indicate their role in the social interaction of the moment. At the same time, by using symbols whose meaning is more or less established by tradition, individuals perpetuate the system of social relations that elicits the symbols themselves.

Thus, a few cultural symbols can be used to define and interpret a great variety of human interactions. Herein lies the secret of social and cultural continuity in the Mayo valley. Development made obsolete the existing cut-and-dried ethnic distinctions. By using the same ethnic terms to define a burgeoning cultural diversity, residents of the valley are able to interpret social relations in a way that ties them to the traditions of the past without rendering the present unintelligible.

Conclusion: Development, Marginality, and Ethnic Identity

The literature on ethnic identity and cultural pluralism is indeed vast. Theories concerning ethnicity range from those that attribute it entirely to structural constraints to those that assert the iron hand of custom as the cause of ethnic diversity. The possibility of ethnic change is implicit in the theories favoring structural variables as causal, for structures do change (Barth 1969). However, the specific ways that cultural symbols and their meanings change are only beginning to be explored (Keyes 1979, 1981; Nagata 1974, 1979), and approaches that are essentially primordialist are by no means dead (see Castile and Kushner 1981). Thus, questions concerning what causes ethnic diversity, how pluralism is maintained, and whether or not ethnicity is innately changeable or immutable remain in the realm of theoretical controversy.

Theories on economic development are less various, although probably not less controversial, than those on ethnic identity. Early development programs had as their theoretical basis the same assumptions about structural variables as some ethnic models: change the economic and political opportunity structure in the correct way, and cultural modernization will follow. Modifications of the goals of development programs have occurred largely in response to moral rather than strictly empirical matters. Uneven growth, and the resulting exclusion of many people from the cultural modernization experienced by a few, offend the spirit of "progress for all," which is an unstated underlying assumption in most development schemes. The cure for the problem of inequality of opportunity has yet to be found, precisely because of the social and cultural effects of early development: new elites refuse to share the bounty, and those who have benefited the least are powerless to insist on their portion.

In the Mayo valley, as in other parts of the world, the theoretical problems concerning both ethnic identity and economic development converge into a single, if ramified, explanatory problem. The issue of ethnic change versus primordialism is complicated by the question of the structural effects of the development program. The empirical facts of human interaction in the region can be cited in support of both kinds of existing theories: social opportunities and structural constraints are important in determining some cultural variables, but symbols and symbolic behaviors serve to bring out the social structure and to give meaning to social relations. These symbols are quite often based on historical customs and manners of specific areas within the valley, although many also encompass the cultural whole. In order to go beyond both structural and primordial theories, it is necessary to focus on the interaction between social opportunities and constraints on the one hand, and cultural symbols on the other. This interaction is not limited to situations like the Mayo valley, but the complexity of life there makes clear the need for a new way of explaining it.

As already noted, the number and variety of social opportunities increased as a result of the government's overall development program. Great wealth was provided to only a few private farmers by irrigation works and government aid, but the granting of ejido lands and the building of schools, clinics, and roads benefited the many. At the same time, new political structures--especially ejido organizations--gave people at least the appearance of political power, if not always the reality.

In general, the overall opportunity structure became more diverse and open as a result of development; however, this diversity in itself led to greater inequality: in a context of upward mobility for some, the lives of many were not significantly improved. For the poor day laborer, life still consists of a long day of work followed by a meal of beans and tortillas and sleep on a woven mat or canvas cot. This is not so different from pre-development life, but this same laborer knows that in the market towns of the valley are the huge mansions of the landowners; these did not exist before development. One legacy of development is a marginalized underclass unable to participate in the new order. Although it does include some people who consider themselves de razón, the greatest part of this underclass is of Mayo ancestry and is culturally Mayo. Here is the "enclave" of Spicer's work and that of his students (e.g. Crumrine 1977, 1981).

Optimists and proponents of the trickle-down theory might hope that the structural changes produced by development will eventually reach these marginal people, but the cruel fact is that Sonora's economy became stagnant in 1970 and shows little sign of recovering. Social opportunities provided by schools, roads, and the like will continue to be felt to some extent, but new opportunities will probably not be forthcoming in the foreseeable future.

The general pattern of development and the lifestyles of those who benefited from it have been well documented (Erasmus 1961; Alcantara 1976). The use of ritual symbols by the marginalized enclave has also been described (Crumrine 1977). The remaining majority of the population in the valley is diverse culturally; this diversity defies explanation by existing paradigms.

The long-term effect of structural change is a cultural continuum between the two extremes. This continuum is made manifest by a variety of cultural symbols that are multivocalic and ambiguous, and thus subject to different interpretations by different people in different situations. Whether or not these symbolic behaviors are seen as ethnic depends on a variety of historical, ecological and personal factors. Social constraints and opportunities vary from community to community. The cultural means of expressing and defining these constraints may be similar in content but different in meaning because of the power of symbols to convey many subtle nuances.

The role of the individual is essential in this scheme of things. The variety of individual behavior in the Mayo region sometimes makes culture seem random and inexplicable, but individuals actually base their behavior and their interpretation of others' behavior on a rather limited set of cultural rules. These rules exist only as a collectivity, for each individual's behavior is based on his own understanding and manipulation of the rules. The rules by themselves cannot predict behavior because of this variety in individual understanding and decisionmaking. Changes in the rules of behavior over time can come about only through changes in individual behavior and in the ways this behavior is interpreted.

The Mayo valley provides an example of how this dialectic between rules and individual behavior works with regard to ethnic identity: before development, there were two ethnic categories that were clearly defined by a set of rules. The effect of development was to create a cultural continuum within which the individual's behavior can vary and be variously understood, depending on the situation. The terms for the ethnic categories have remained basically the same, but the ways of expressing and interpreting the rules that establish these categories are in the process of expansion. This process is by no means anomic, and residents of the valley demonstrate the human tendency toward systematic rather than chaotic change. How the rules combine and how individuals behave vary from community to community. The research on which this work is based was conducted in only a few of these communities, albeit they exhibit a variety of social opportunities and constraints. The continuity of cultural rules from one community to the other provides the key to an understanding of ethnicity and ethnic change in general.

3

Ethnic Symbols in the Mayo Valley

Ethnic Symbols and Social Behavior

Despite the disparity in informants' descriptions of what makes a Mayo and what a Mestizo, it is possible to identify certain traits and behaviors that all agree are either Mayo or Mestizo. The combination of Mayo and Mestizo traits and behaviors, or the ability to switch from one set of behaviors to the other, characterizes those in the middle of the continuum. This ability to manipulate ethnic symbols according to social circumstances makes for participation by individuals from all along the spectrum in social events defined as either Mayo or Mestizo.

One of the most confusing ethnic traits is that of surname. This confusion results from the fact that, in a setting of cultural flux, surnames cannot be changed. Last names are an indication of ancestry but not necessarily of present-day identity or behavior. Typical Mayo names are Buitimea, Jupamea, Moroyoqui, and the like. To a knowledgeable person, these are quite distinct from Spanish names such as González and Acosta. Having one or more Mayo surnames is usually seen as a Mayo trait. However, one of the more popular musical bands in the region is not ashamed to advertise the Mayo surname of its members. On the other hand, having two Spanish surnames is not necessarily a Mestizo trait. One of the few monolingual Mayo speakers I met had the surnames of two prominent families whose ancestors helped build the town of Alamos. At the same time, surname cannot be ignored as at least a possible ethnic indicator. The comment by a middle-class Huatabampo resident that "any Moroyoqui" could lay claim to private land under the Echeverría administration illustrates the role of Mayo surnames in identifying Indian-ness and a concomitant rural poverty.

Beyond surnames, it is language that provides individuals with the symbols of ethnic identity, one of which is language use itself. Over 90% of native Mayo-speakers are bilingual in Spanish (INI Census 1976). The reverse is not true, however: those who learn Spanish at their mothers' knees do not go on to learn Mayo as a second language. This is primarily because knowledge of Mayo is generally a low-prestige symbol not desirable to Spanish-speakers even in this changeable ethnic arena. Spanish-speakers growing up in close proximity to Mayo-speakers usually pick up some Mayo, and some understand more than they can speak. In general, however, knowledge of Mayo on the part of native Spanish-speakers is limited to a few obscenities.

Bilingualism in itself exists on something of a continuum, as few people are fully bilingual. Mayo-speakers as a rule speak Mayo better than they do Spanish, and there is a distinctive accent identifiable in the Spanish of many whose first language is Mayo. Nevertheless, bilingualism is an important aspect of the cultural continuum, for it allows people to conform to the requirements of both Mayo and Mestizo social situations. To be sure, the person speaking Spanish with a Mayo accent is not so fully accepted in Mestizo situations, and the Spanish-speaker who knows only a few Mayo words is usually ignored in Mayo situations. Even minimal bilingual ability, however, is better than none at all.

Language-speaking ability and surname are, to a large extent, circumstances of birth and early childhood which are difficult to change. The other two behaviors that are among the clearest ethnic indicators are more subject to individual choice and manipulation. Participating in a major way in the Mayo folk-Catholic system represents a substantial commitment to Mayo identity. It also requires full Mayo-speaking ability. Pressure from family members and fear of divine punishment contribute substantially to an individual's decision to fulfill a major vow or become a religious leader, but in the final analysis it is up to the individual to decide whether, and when, to do so.

A distinct cultural symbol discussed extensively by N. Ross Crumrine (1964) is the house cross. This is a wooden cross found in the patios of many Mayo houses. It is decorated on the Day of the Dead, and there are several other household rituals in which this cross plays a part. In my survey, I found that households with house crosses all year were undeniably Mayo. However, a substantial number of self-identified Mayos, including some important ritual performers, did not have house crosses. A third category, those households that place crosses in their yards only during Holy Week, is an example of the compromise behavior characteristic of the middle of the cultural spectrum. Although both major participation in the fiesta system and the use of the house-cross are examples of folk-Catholic behavior, the two are clearly distinct in the extent of commitment to Mayo identity implied.

Individuals who have Mayo surnames, speak Mayo, participate fully in the Mayo religious system, and live in a house with a house cross throughout the year are clearly on the Mayo extreme of the cultural continuum. Those who have Spanish surnames, are monolingual in Spanish, participate only marginally or not at all in the Mayo folk-religious system, and never have house crosses in their patios are at the Mestizo end of the continuum. The startling cultural array between the two extremes derives in large part from a combination of traits and behaviors drawn from these extremes, or the ability to play up or play down those behaviors in specific social contexts. When economic factors are added into this construct, the possibilities for variety are greater still.

The people at the Mayo end of the cultural continuum continue to practice their traditions because they have been shut out of the economic and social opportunity ladder brought about by development. These people see their culture, with its rich religious tapestry and its deep-rooted traditions, as preferable to the culture practiced by non-Mayos at the same economic level. It must not be assumed that everyone at the bottom of the economic scale is also at the Mayo extreme of the cultural continuum, for many of the poorest are people who came to the valley looking for wealth, only to find more poverty.

Those people, both natives and newcomers, who found social opportunities, have taken advantage of them with various degrees of success. People of Mayo ancestry are included in this group; to the extent that they are successful, they tend to emulate their well-to-do neighbors and downplay their Mayo background. Even this pattern of ethnic change accompanying economic change has its exceptions, however; in the village of Buaysiacobe, comparative wealth and Mayo identity are found in conjunction. At the Mestizo extreme, few people of Mayo ancestry are to be found. However, this is not to say that class and ethnicity are interchangeable. That is, although the wealthiest people in any given community are clearly Mestizo today, this is also true of many of the poorest. The descendants of Totoliguoqui are excluded from great wealth, but they are not the only poor residents of the valley.

It is the ability of individuals toward the middle of the cultural spectrum to change their behavior that makes for the emergence of situational ethnicity. The same situations can be defined differently in different communities. In one community, ejido meetings are Mestizo and everyone speaks Spanish. In another, ejido meetings are ethnically neutral and both Mayo and Spanish are used. In one community, conversion to Protestantism is a declaration of ethnic change, while in another it is ethnically meaningless. These distinctions in how situations are defined are produced primarily by historical factors, as shown in the discussions of specific communities in Chapters Five, Six, and Seven.

There are two types of situations, however, that are universally recognized. One is that of the market towns of Huatabampo and Navojoa; here, everyone who can speaks Spanish. The other clear situation is observation of the rituals of Mayo folk-Catholicism. Here, Mayo is de rigueur, and a knowledge of the rituals and their meanings is necessary to anyone who wishes to be recognized as a full participant in the system. Those displaying a lack of such knowledge are ridiculed and in some cases scorned as outsiders. On the other hand, many people who do not speak Mayo participate in the religious system in a minor way, by making and fulfilling vows that require less ritual and linguistic competence.

Three of the four Mayo ethnic indicators are included in the Mayo religious system: knowledge of Mayo, being a major participant in the rituals, and having a permanent house cross. Thus, an understanding of the ritual system is essential to comprehending how ethnicity is displayed, concealed, or changed in the Mayo region in general.

Mayo and Orthodox Catholicism

In a broad sense, Mayo religion is a type of folk-Catholicism. Folk-Catholicism is a combination of elements from the orthodox Catholic liturgy with elements from local folk beliefs, deities, and rituals. Although missionaries have often frowned on folk-Catholicism, the Church in some of its laws has countenanced the inclusion of local beliefs, so long as they do not threaten orthodoxy. This flexibility has been largely responsible for the success of the Church over time and space. Participants in the Mayo system believe quite strongly that they are Catholics; some even say that it is the Mestizos who are not. There is general recognition that the Catholicism practiced in the churches of the market towns differs from the Mayo version, but the differences are rarely brought up or questioned. The orthodox priest is called in for a few of the more important aspects of some Mayo rituals, but the priests themselves understand little of what their actions mean to the other performers in these ceremonies.

For the most part, these ceremonies are conducted by a lay minister, called a *maestro*, who understands the ceremonies as completely as anyone. Maestros are apprenticed as young men (and occasionally women), and are taught all the prayers and rituals by participating in those conducted by the maestro in charge. The prayers are entirely derived from the orthodox Catholic liturgy, but the rituals are combinations of orthodox and specifically Mayo features. There are often two maestros at any important ceremony, one senior and one junior or apprentice.

There is no specific point at which an apprentice becomes a full-fledged maestro. People begin to request his services at smaller rituals such as funerals, and he is gradually accorded the title of maestro. There is no ceremony to mark the change in status. Maestros are paid according to the extent of their services and the wealth of those requesting them. There is some competition among maestros, who are selected for any given ritual on the basis of past performances, availability, and to some extent association with a specific village church. There is no formal relationship between maestro and congregation such as is seen in the parochial system of the orthodox Church.

In any ceremony, there are performers who must pay the maestros and the other performers; there are also people who participate without either paying or being paid. Each of these categories is clearly defined by the unwritten rules of the ceremonial system, which has as its basis the belief that personal or family calamity can be overcome by means of vows to saints. If the crisis--usually sickness or accident--is solved in a satisfactory way by whatever means available, the vow must be completed. Its completion almost always involves a ritual in which money, food, or goods must be given to others. Alternatively, dancing or some other kind of ritual performance in public is required. Often, a combination of both performance and material contribution is involved.

The practice of making vows to saints is well known in the formal Catholic system, but the completion of the vow is almost invariably a personal event. There is no public ceremony organized expressly for the completion of vows, at least among the laity. Participants in the Mayo system also make minor promises that are fulfilled personally by the individual, but by far the most important events of the ceremonial system are occasions for the public fulfillment of vows. These fiestas externally resemble those of southern Mexico, but the latter are carried out primarily in order to gain prestige and authority. It is true that the Mayo sponsor gains prestige within a small circle of kin and friends, but the main reason for Mayo sponsorship is the fear that God will punish the recalcitrant or some member of his kin group. Most vows are not made by the sick person but by a relative, usually a parent. Not to fulfill the vow, therefore, is a sign of disrespect to kin as well as to God. These two forces--kin and God--are among the most persuasive elements of the motivational systems of almost all rural peoples, and Mayos are no exception.

Major Participants and Ceremonies

Major participants include those who fulfill major vows such as being a fiesta sponsor or a ritual dancer, and those who are paid to perform the public ceremonies associated with this fulfillment. Apart from the maestro, there are three types of paid performers: *pascolas*, deer dancers, and musicians. Each of these is paid approximately three times the daily wages earned by *jornaleros*. There is also a great deal of prestige involved in performing: the paid performers are, so to speak, the stars of the fiesta. Many aspects of the fiestas are ignored or not well understood, but people from all along the cultural continuum flock to see the dancers and listen to their ribald jokes, even though only the Mayo-speakers can understand them. The performers must dance and play all night for up to three nights, depending on the importance of the fiesta. The sponsors of the fiesta must supply, in addition to the pay for each performer, food and unlimited quantities of *mescal*, a strong liquor made from the maguey cactus. This, it is thought, keeps the performers from falling asleep.

The pascola and deer dances are quite distinct, and usually the deer dancer performs with a different set of musicians from those accompanying the pascolas. Both types of dances are usually held in a *ramada*, a structure with a thatch roof and no sides, affording both shade and breeze. The dancers are rarely in the church, and their characteristic dancing is never done in the church. This probably betokens the aboriginal derivation of these performances: the pascola music may be played on instruments of European origin, but there is nothing remotely resembling dancers with animal masks and cocoon-rattle leggings in the orthodox Catholic liturgy.

The word *pasco'ola* means "old man of the fiesta" in Mayo, and without at least one pascola there can be no fiesta. At church fiestas there are always three or more. There is never more than one deer dancer, and smaller fiestas have none. When not involved in their formal tasks, these performers are to be found making coarse jokes about various aspects of the fiesta and the other performers. These jokes are always in Mayo. Although the pascolas are theoretically the only individuals allowed to indulge in vulgar humor during the fiesta solemnities, fiesta-goers in advanced stages of inebriation have been known to take part with impunity in the antics of pascolas.

There are usually three musicians for the pascolas and four for the deer dancer, although at large fiestas there are two sets of pascola musicians who alternate playing. The musicians tend to be a more solemn and sober group than the dancers, but musicians by no means abstain from drinking. They do not engage in joking to the extent that the dancers do, and their participation in general is less obvious than that of the flamboyant dancers.

Beals (1945:127) reports a myth about how these performers acquire their calling. It was said that the seeker entered a cave in the sierra and was swallowed by a huge snake. After being passed through the snake's anus, he was in the snake cave, where another large snake wrapped around the aspirant. If, after these ordeals, he was unafraid, he was allowed to choose from the wall of the cave the regalia of a pascola, deer dancer, or musician.

Today, there is still some attempt to shroud in mystery the origin of a performer's vocation. In actuality it derives, like that of the maestro's, from apprenticeship at an early age. Pascolas and especially musicians tend to pass their special knowledge and talent on to sons and nephews. The deer dancer's is more of a personal calling, sometimes originating with a vow, and does not run in families. With the exception of this small number of deer dancers, the paid performers do not participate because of vows. Their vocation, on the other hand, is permanent, although some retire from practice. They are specialists hired by the fiesta sponsors, and it is their knowledge that helps keep the system operating: they are ongoing, while the sponsors are temporary. When not participating in ceremonies, these men are usually day laborers, indistinguishable from others of their employment. Their religious status is known, but makes little impact on daily life.

Of all the vows possible in response to crisis, those of fiesta sponsorship carry by far the greatest amount of responsibility and expense. If the maestros and paid performers provide ongoing special knowledge and talents, the fiesta sponsors, called *fiesteros*, are vital to the system in that they provide the occasion for the expression of that knowledge. The enormous expenditures made by fiesteros and their families make possible the continuation of the fiestas as they are traditionally carried out. The extent to which fiesta sponsors continue to bear this burden defines the extent to which the traditional fiestas will continue or will change.

There are two basic types of fiestas: church fiestas and house fiestas, known as *velaciones*. The church fiestas are much more elaborate and longer, and they feature at least 4 and as many as 14 sponsors. Church fiesteros have duties beyond the actual fiesta. They must appear each Sunday to clean the church and to perform specific Sunday services conducted by the maestro. The maestro is contracted and paid each year by that year's fiesteros; he is then committed to preside over all the rituals associated with fiesteros for that year.

The length of fiesta sponsorship varies from one year to three, depending on the village. Likewise, the number of fiestas celebrated each year, and the consequent expense of sponsorship, vary from church to church. The elaborateness of these rituals, and the amount of food and other goods required of each church's fiesteros, differ, just as the numbers of fiesteros and fiestas do: the church with the most fiesteros also has the most fiestas and requires the largest expenditure at each one. In cases where fiesteros have three-year vows, these are completed one year at a time at long intervals. Even so, no fiestero is expected to amass alone the amount of money required for sponsorship. He or she is helped by relatives and friends. This help extends to performing duties: often a relative will stand in for the fiestero at Sunday ceremonies.

The house fiestas are smaller, and are part of the tradition in which the crucifix or an image of a saint is removed from its church and carried from hamlet to hamlet in a rough circle around the village where the church is located. The itinerary is arranged well in advance, and is determined by who will be sponsoring velaciones in which hamlet. The saint spends each night in a different house, and each house provides food for the hamlet-dwellers who attend the velación as well as for those who accompany the saint. The actual sponsor of the velación must perform special rituals, conducted by the maestro, at the special altar constructed for the saint in each house. All those attending the velación also pray the rosary, led by the maestro.

This pattern of velaciones generally occurs around Lent, when the crucifixes of all the Mayo churches are carried around the countryside in the company of *fariseos*, ritual clowns associated with Lent. At least four other images of saints in the region enjoy a more limited popularity but are also carried from hamlet to hamlet and honored with house fiestas.

Velación sponsors almost always have three-year vows. In the third year, the velación should be grander, and should include at least one pascola. Smaller velaciones may do without. The amount of money expended on velaciones varies more widely than that for the church fiestas, for which each village specifies the quantity of food and money required of each fiestero; noncompliance with this standard means that the promise is not fulfilled. There is a certain amount of competition among velación sponsors, especially within the same hamlet, to give the best velación, for these are social as well as ritual affairs. Supernatural sanctions on stinginess are absent, however.

In the context of the fiesta, the uninitiated may make few distinctions among the various performers except to notice their variety. The fariseos and another group, the *matachines*, appear to be dancers and jokesters similar to the pascolas, but with different costumes. The major difference between them is that pascolas are paid professionals, while matachines and fariseos participate because of religious vows. All three groups must provide their own costumes, and fariseos contribute small amounts of money for the fiesta at the end of Lent. Neither the matachín nor the fariseo vow demands the amount of money and energy involved in sponsoring a fiesta. However, making one of these vows and deciding to fulfill it is one of the clearest Mayo symbolic behaviors, because of the effort involved and especially because of the public nature of the fulfillment. The individual who participates in this major way in the folk-religious system is announcing to the world a commitment to Mayo ethnic identity.

Matachines are usually associated with the dead; they are supposed to dance at any funeral near their homes and at the anniversaries of deaths. This role is now usually carried out only if the deceased was a matachín or a very revered person. The dancing of the matachines today is for the most part limited to the day of the fiesta of the patron saint to whom the vow was made, and the Day of the Dead (November 2).

Fariseos represent the soldiers who persecuted Jesus during Holy Week. They also are purported to be devils and, at the same time, protectors of the crucifix during Lent. This is the only time that fariseos appear in rituals. They wear enormous goatskin masks and are dressed in vaguely military attire. Each carries a wooden knife and a long wooden spear; these are brandished at will during the ceremonies. Fariseos themselves may misbehave, and are expected to perform such antics as mimicking copulation, satirizing the solemnity of other performers, frightening children, and in general entertaining the people involved in the Lenten ceremonies. At the same time, they are expected to maintain order and enforce the rules of conduct they themselves break with wild abandon. Fariseos are organized along military lines, with corporals, captains, and, at the head of the group, the *pilatos*, who represent Pontius Pilate during the Holy Week rituals.

Minor Promises and Ceremonies

There are several other types of vows associated with Lent and Easter; none of these requires the outlay of time and effort expected of fariseos. These vows also do not require knowledge of the Mayo language, and the ritual knowledge needed to fulfill them is not as complex. Individuals who make these minor vows may be found all along the cultural continuum, especially in the villages of the region. Thus, although the system is universally regarded as Mayo, people who otherwise would identify themselves as de razón do participate in minor ways in the religious fiestas. By their participation, these individuals help to validate a Mayo ethnic situation by behaving in as Mayo a way as possible. At the same time, it is here that the uniquely Mayo system overlaps with the orthodox system, for some of the minor vows completed in the Mayo churches are also found in churches throughout Mexico.

Verónicas are young women who carry the crucifix from hamlet to hamlet during Lent; in a sense, they are the female equivalent of fariseos, but much less flamboyant. Small children also participate in the Friday Lent services in each church. The girls are called *tres marías* (Three Marys) and the boys *tres reyes* (Three Kings).

Apart from these vows, which are carried out only during the Lenten ceremonies, there are numerous vows to the seemingly innumerable saints in the Mayo region. These promises range from taking flowers to a specific saint to playing band music in the procession of a saint or dancing before a saint at a specific time. Some of these vows, feature *hábitos*, colorful but simple garments donned in a ritual before a saint with the blessing of the maestro and the help of godparents.

The number and variety of vows make for an extremely complex ritual system. Not all saints are known to all people, however. There is a tendency to make vows to certain saints, depending on the individual's residence or birthplace. If the mother of a sick child was born in the lower Mayo valley, she will probably make a vow to the patron of her natal village, even though she lives in the northwest region. On the other hand, most residents of the latter area make vows to the patron saints of the Navojoa or San Pedro churches.

Church Leadership and Structure

There are two kinds of religious structures: churches and chapels. Chapels may have patron saints with small fiestas, and some have a few fiesteros. Only churches have fariseos and the elaborate Lenten ceremonies they perform. Because of their small size, chapels have only one elected leader, the president. He maintains the chapel, using alms brought by believers to the saints. He also has the right to any money left over after maintenance costs. Churches, on the other hand, have an entire council, which is elected by the village and charged with maintenance as well as with communication with other church councils concerning the various exchanges of rituals that characterize the ceremonial system in the valley as a whole. The church council is allowed to divide up the remaining alms after necessary expenses have been covered.

As may be expected, this system can be the source of a great deal of animosity among council members, as well as between them and the community at large, especially in villages where substantial amounts of money are given by the faithful. Nevertheless, it provides a structure of authority and assures that order is maintained on the church premises. This structure may have arisen in response to the religious turbulence of the 1930s, during which Mestizos raided Mayo churches and burned the sacred images of the saints.

The Fiesta System

The Mayo ceremonial year follows the orthodox Catholic calendar closely; the feast-day of the patron saint is the occasion for the major fiesta of the year in each church. Likewise, the Lenten ceremonies correspond in time to those of the orthodox Catholic rituals. It is in content that the ceremonies differ.

A typical fiesta for the church's patron saint begins three days before the actual saint's day. The fiesteros and their kin have already built temporary kitchens in a prescribed pattern in the traditional kitchen area. Each kitchen consists of an open adobe hearth, a ramada, and an enclosed hut where the fiestero's family sleeps; each fiestero has his or her own kitchen, and these are in a row, with common walls separating the enclosed portions. Each kitchen also has a table and benches, where paid performers and relatives of the fiesteros eat the food prepared on the hearth. There are certain foods required for the fiesta, notably *guacabaqui* (beef stew), *bannari* (corn pudding), and wheat bread. There is always food available, and in theory all who go to the fiesta eat this sacred food. It is considered a grave insult to refuse food at the fiesta. In actuality, the opportunity to refuse food is rare, for it is seldom offered, and those who are entitled to eat know very well who they are: relatives and close friends of the fiestero. Those who invite themselves out of order are of course fed, but are held in contempt.

On the night the fiesta opens, the dancers and musicians arrive in trucks rented by the fiesteros--many of the performers come from as far as 50 kilometers away from the host village. The pascolas and the three head fiesteros exchange formal greetings in Mayo, fireworks are set off, and the fiesta begins. The performers are fed, and at around 10 p.m. they begin to dance. This continues until dawn, when everyone rests in the kitchens. Later in the morning, the image of the saint whose fiesta is being celebrated is taken from the church by the fiesteros and carried in a procession to a traditional spot outside the village where it is to meet the saint from another village church or chapel. The churches and many of the chapels display colorful flags, which serve as identity symbols. Each year at the patron saint's fiesta there is a new flag, blessed in advance by a Mestizo priest in Huatabampo or Navojoa.

At the meeting place, the paid dancers perform; matachines might also take part. When the fiesteros from the visiting village arrive with their saint and their flag, formal greetings are exchanged; this is done entirely in Mayo. After more dancing, the two sets of fiesteros return to the fiesta church, and install both saints on the decorated altars prepared for them. The dancers and fiesteros march to the ramada outside the church, and the head pascola prays to the saint. After this ritual, all the participants retire to the kitchens to eat and sleep. At this time, and during the next 24 hours, people who have promised to take flowers, candles, and so forth to the saint have the opportunity to fulfill those vows; hábitos are also donned during this period.

The evening before the actual saint's day is the most important time in the fiesta. In the early evening there are rituals and prayers led by the maestro, followed by the fiesteros' flag ritual. Attendance by people with minor vows or those who come to pray to the saint is at its peak; the church is full of people, and the altar is decorated with flowers and candles. In the ramada, the pascolas and deer dancer dance all night.

On the final day of the fiesta, a general tone of exhaustion prevails. Nevertheless, several important events occur. If the celebration is for the day of the patron saint, the fiesteros pass their offices on to the next year's sponsors. This is done through the Mestizo priest, who also sometimes says Mass. The priest takes the ceremonial rosary from around each fiestero's neck and places it around the incoming replacement's neck; he also transfers the other symbols of office. The new fiesteros then perform the flag ceremony with the new flag. The priest leaves, and the maestro conducts the closing ceremonies. These are followed by other closing ceremonies in front of the ramada, led by the pascolas. The visiting fiesteros leave, carrying their saint in procession.

After these ceremonies, both old and new fiesteros go to the kitchens, where the outgoing fiesteros present food and goods to the incoming ones. The amount of food and material given away varies from village to village. Each new fiestero then gives most of the food received to specifically designated individuals, usually relatives. Tradition holds that this is the *amarre*, or tying down, of those who receive the food: they are committed to bring twice as much as they receive to the following year's fiesta. In this way the burden of fiesta sponsorship is divided among the fiesteros' kin, although the commitment is not always honored in full.

The pattern of fiestas varies somewhat in the amount of expense involved and in the details of some of the ceremonies. They also differ in the number of people who attend. In general, the patron saint's fiesta is the most elaborate ritually, entails the greatest expense, and has the largest attendance. It is also invariably accompanied by a secular fiesta: carnival rides, shooting galleries, food stands, and other entertainments are as characteristic of most fiestas as are the pascolas. Fiestas also feature secular dances, and the music from electric guitars often drowns out the violins of the musicians in the ramada.

Although the religious and secular aspects of the fiesta are conceptually different, they are both integral aspects of the event. The vast majority of participants, including fiesteros, see no blasphemy in the gaudy carnival rides. Indeed, everyone who can afford it pays for some kind of secular entertainment; those who cannot pay look on in vicarious enjoyment. In fact, the rides and games are said to attract people to the fiesta, and the informal competition among villages over which has the "biggest" fiesta makes this attraction an important one. The games also bring proceeds to the village, for each concession must pay the village treasury for the privilege of using the community grounds. In some villages, funds from the community treasury now help pay the religious performers; in others, donations from the concessions are requested directly by the fiesteros to help defray the costs of the fiesta. As one fiestero put it, without the religious fiesta there would be no reason for the carnival. This illustrates the extent to which the two are seen as inseparable.

Lent and Easter Ceremonies

Lent is one of the most pleasant times of the year in Sonora. The nights can be cold, but the days are comparatively mild. The winter rains have ended, and many of the desert plants are in flower. The cottonwood trees along the river are full of new green leaves, as are the mesquite trees in the thorn forest and the villages. The wheat and safflower fields, too, are a brilliant green. At this time the fields do not require much attention, so many jornaleros are employed but rarely, and ejidatarios have a certain amount of leisure time. It is small wonder, then, that the Lenten rituals are so popular: the countryside is blooming, the weather is pleasant, and the people have time on their hands.

The ceremonies begin on the first Friday in Lent, at the village church. Here, the fariseos gather, dressed in their costumes; their number varies from 20 to 300, depending on the church. The Friday ceremony, called the *conti*, is conducted by a maestro paid by the fariseos. The conti is an elaborate version of the orthodox Catholic stations of the cross, a ritual practiced throughout the world. While wearing their masks, the fariseos are forbidden to speak, providing an excellent reason for the explicit pantomimes so characteristic of their behavior. Fariseos also see that the people conducting the ceremony are appropriately solemn and orderly. After praying at each cross, the procession returns to the church. The fariseos then prepare to leave for the round of velaciones scheduled for that week.

Only a few of the fariseos go out each week; in this way the burden of the vow is reduced. The pilatos and captains likewise divide their responsibility. They decide which fariseos will go out each week, and they coordinate the various activities entailed in traveling through the countryside with a group of masked men given to outrageous behavior. The leaders are also in charge of the alms collected during these peregrinations. At each hamlet along the route of the velaciones, the fariseos visit each house, beating their drums and collecting alms. The verónicas are in charge of carrying the crucifix and the alms box, but the pilatos and captains are responsible for the money collected. This is carefully counted and recorded, and is used to pay the maestro and to cover the cost of the fiesta on Easter Sunday. Each Friday the fariseos return with the crucifix to the church. The following week a different set of fariseos continues the round of velaciones. The last one or two velaciones are held in the village proper.

When discussing their vows, fariseos stress the sacredness of the promise and the onerous nature of its fulfillment: the mask is heavy, the nights are cold, they must walk long distances, and so on. Their behavior tells a different story. They must walk long distances, it is true, but walking is the prevalent means of travel for all the poor of the valley. The fariseos, furthermore, travel in highly visible groups of mischief-makers. From one point of view, their supposedly arduous travels have all the appearances of a protracted lark. They leave home and its responsibilities to walk about the landscape, entertaining the populace in the company of their friends. They are fed regularly and at no cost, although they do many chores at the velaciones. In short, the fulfillment of this sacred vow has its lighter side. It is perhaps for this reason that the number of fariseos has not decreased in response to economic development in the area.

The Holy Week ceremonies are a culmination of Lent, just as in the orthodox Church. The Mayo rituals vary from church to church, but the basic elements are the same. They feature a re-enactment of the biblical story of the arrest, crucifixion, and resurrection of Jesus. There are a few Mayo twists to this ritual drama, but for the most part it is merely an extremely elaborate version of the Catholic liturgy. The ceremonies have been described minutely by Beals (1945:155-161) and N.Ross Crumrine (1977:85-97), but a brief outline of the festivities is in order here.

On Wednesday there is a *tinieblas* ceremony, whose major feature is darkness. This is a version of the orthodox ritual in which the altars of the church are stripped in preparation for the remaining rituals. Thursday evening is the *corrida del viejito*, portraying the search and discovery of Jesus by Roman soldiers (played by fariseos). The ceremony, conducted at dusk, can be extremely rowdy, and is sometimes frighteningly similar to the mob scenes described in the Bible.

Friday afternoon is the most elaborate ritual in all of Mayo ceremonialism. The church fills with people, and the participants are dressed in their finest. At one side of the church is a bier decorated with white lace and flowers. At the other side is a hut made of new green leaves, with the large church crucifix inside. After many hours of praying, during which time hábitos are donned and other minor promises fulfilled, the fariseos "kill" Jesus with their wooden knives. The body is removed from the crucifix and placed in the bier. A conti follows. That night, there is a second and in some churches a third conti in which the bier and the Virgin take different routes through the village and meet at a prescribed point. The church remains open all night, and the fariseos guard the bier, which is surrounded by lighted candles.

The Mayo belief is that Jesus rose from the dead on Saturday, not Sunday. At dawn on Saturday, the pascolas or the maestro announce that Jesus has risen. The "body" is removed from the bier and returned to the cross. Meanwhile, a curtain is drawn across one third of the church. When the church has filled with people and the fariseos are lined up along two sides of the church, the pascolas emerge suddenly from behind the curtain, shout "Gloria!" and run out of the church. This is repeated three times. The fariseos are then baptized, to exonerate them for their persecution and murder of Jesus. Their masks are burned and the Easter fiesta begins, with pascolas and deer dancers as well as fiesta food provided by the fariseos. This fiesta lasts all night, and in most churches is ended by simple closing ceremonies on Sunday.

At Júpare, the church with the most elaborate ceremonials, there is a re-enactment on Sunday of the biblical scene in which John tells Mary, the mother of Jesus that her son has risen from the dead. This is a very joyful ceremony. The fariseos, *sans* masks and dressed in their fanciest clothes, preside over this renewal ritual, which ends with the participants gleefully breaking numerous confetti-filled eggs over each other's heads.

Conclusion

The continued variety and complexity of the Mayo religious system indicate that its role in the lives of the participants is not moribund. The fact that some of the ceremonies, notably the Lent and Easter rituals, involve the active participation of hundreds of people in each village demonstrates an ongoing interest in the system. The basic motivating forces of that system are certainly not likely to disappear soon. Illness and accident are common, and the use of modern medicine complements rather than replaces the making of vows. Kin sanctions against refusals to complete a vow are undoubtedly going to continue, and supernatural sanctions are believed in by Mestizo and Mayo alike.

Although ostensibly Catholic, the Mayo ceremonies have enough unique elements to be considered distinctly Mayo. The greater part of the rituals are in the Mayo language, and the participants must speak Mayo in order to understand their roles. Indeed, knowing Mayo is probably essential even to the onlooker's full understanding of the rituals. The pascola jokes are in Mayo, and Mayo is the predominant language spoken in nonritual conversations during the fiesta. People who speak Spanish well proudly converse in Mayo on these occasions, while those who do not speak Mayo are ridiculed as traitors to their ancestry.

There is, however, enough similarity between orthodox Catholicism and the Mayo system to allow for a certain area of ambivalence, or blurring, between them. The central roles in the fiestas are played by people who identify themselves and are identified by others as Mayos. Minor vows, made by people all along the cultural continuum, are completed in Mayo churches and with the help of Mayo maestros.

Language use is an important means of identifying the fiestas as Mayo. This is true of other special social events, such as ejido meetings in some villages. More to the point is the issue of which language is used in daily life, and here the matter becomes complicated. Most Mayo-speakers are bilingual. To be sure, some speak better Spanish than others, but most speak it acceptably. Therefore they speak the language most suited to a given situation. The fiesta demands Mayo. The ejido meeting usually elicits Spanish. Conversations with neighbors are often carried on in a mixture of both. This variety of linguistic behavior gives a clue to the complexity of ethnic behavior in general: the same individual may be a fariseo and an ejidatario; at the fiesta he is Mayo, but when dealing with bank officials he will do his best to appear Mestizo. At home he may speak to his wife in Mayo and his children in Spanish.

This description of language behavior illustrates the situational nature of ethnic identity in southern Sonora. In Huatabampo, the Mayo country bumpkins do their best to appear Mestizo. At the fiestas, people whose knowledge of Mayo does not exceed a few sentences proudly display their limited ability. In many situations, ethnic identity is not important; here, a natural mixture of traits is to be found. Of course, people on the extreme ends of the ethnic continuum cannot play this game, for their resources are limited. Still, they do their best. One bank official, when visiting an ejido and surrounded by Mayos, told me he was Mayo. When pressed, he admitted that his definition of Mayo extended to all those born in the Mayo valley; this category was broad enough to include even him.

Individual behavior, then, varies along a cultural continuum and according to specific situations. In every case, the individual manipulates available cultural resources in order to obtain specific goals. Thus, each individual's motivation is the basis for the inevitable variety of ethnic behavior. Beyond mere individual manipulation of rules determined by situations, however, is the larger context of economic and social variety in the Mayo region. Clearly, though there are certain situations found throughout the area, the social contexts of the densely populated lower Mayo differ greatly from the region outside the irrigation district, and both these areas differ from the area northwest of the river. The differences in economic and social opportunities in these three regions determine to a large extent the differences in individual responses. These, in turn, make for distinctions in ethnic behavior. In order to explain these distinctions, it is necessary to explore the differences in contexts and the variety of responses in specific communities in the three regions.

4

Ecology, Politics, and Economy in the Mayo Area

Introduction

The Sonoran Mayo country lies about 800 kilometers from the United States-Mexico border at Nogales. South of the border, the international highway traverses several ecological zones, but the entire region belongs to the vast Sonoran desert and is characteristically arid. South of the seaport of Guaymas, the natural vegetation is dense thorn forest, comprised of bright green mesquite trees and tall organ-pipe cacti as well as many other varieties of desert plants. This environment is the same as that aboriginally inhabited by the Mayos and still inhabited by most Yaquis.

About 250 kilometers south of Guaymas is Ciudad Obregón, a bustling city of over 100,000 and the major urban center for the Yaqui and Mayo valleys. It is here that many of the harvested crops are stored and processed before being transported to other parts of Mexico. There is little industry in Obregón, but commerce and agricultural processing are important parts of the city's economy. Mestizo residents of towns as far away as Huatabampo regularly visit Obregón for shopping and entertainment, but many of the poor have never seen the city. The modern buildings and wide streets of Obregón, as well as the enormous residences of Mestizos grown wealthy from agriculture, provide an extreme contrast to the tiny hamlets of wattle-and-daub houses characteristic of most rural settlements.

South of Obregón are the broad fields of wheat and safflower that have made the region famous. The Yaqui river Irrigation District extends south almost to the Mayo river itself, and it is difficult to determine by observation where the Yaqui district ends and the Mayo begins. Most of the fields are owned by Mestizos, but there are a considerable number of ejidos, with members representing all points on the cultural continuum, in the Yaqui Irrigation District. It is here that all of the collective ejidos were established in the final weeks of the Echeverría administration, and there are people from the Mayo valley who are members of these ejidos also.

Fifty kilometers southeast of Obregón is the city of Navojoa, situated on the Mayo river. One of the original Mayo pueblos, Navojoa now has a population of over 40,000, mostly Mestizo. The city is a smaller version of Obregón and, like it, has a sleek and modern aspect. The largest buildings are banks and agricultural machinery showrooms. If it were not for the signs in Spanish, one might take it to be a city in California's Central Valley.

Once in Navojoa, one has arrived in the Mayo country, although few tourists driving through the city on their way to the quainter and cooler south realize that there is any Indian population in the vicinity. Most of that population is to be found in the region south and west of Navojoa, along the now mostly dry riverbed. The density of the population of those on the Mayo extreme of the continuum increases toward the mouth of the river (INI 1976), where the major historic town of Santa Cruz once stood.

Huatabampo, a town of 10,000 located several kilometers east of the site of Santa Cruz, now performs the functions that town once served. Like the larger cities of the region, Huatabampo is inexorably modern in design: enormous stone and brick homes situated along broad, paved streets are the distinguishing features of the center of town, and the municipio headquarters are housed in a large square stone building with none of the arches and curves characteristic of traditional Mexican architecture. This modern aspect of the central part of the town quickly tapers off into unpaved streets with smaller houses; on the outskirts, wattle-and-daub huts are common. These structures, along with the great number of horses and horse-carts, evince Huatabampo's proximity to the rural zone, where poverty imposes a more modest way of life.

Huatabampo is predominantly Mestizo: although one may frequently hear conversations in Mayo on the street-corners, the speakers are generally in town on business from outlying hamlets. That business is firmly in the hands of Mestizo merchants, bankers, and government agents. There are also some Mayo-speakers living in the poorer sections of Huatabampo, but in general they work in the fields surrounding the town or in packing houses where winter vegetables are crated for export to the United State. They are not to be found in the grandiose houses on the paved streets, except as maids or gardeners.

Political Organization

Each state in Mexico is divided into political entities known as municipios, roughly corresponding to counties in the United States. Each municipio has a *cabecera*, equivalent to a county seat. The bulk of the population still clearly Mayo lives mainly in three municipios: Huatabampo, Etchojoa, and Navojoa (INI 1977); the cabeceras are the towns bearing the same names as the municipios. The elected leaders of the municipios oversee the appointment of *comisarios de policia* (police chiefs) in larger villages, and *delegados de policia* (police deputies) in smaller hamlets. These officials maintain order in their areas of jurisdiction. The municipio cabecera's control of the countryside does not go much beyond this. *Consejos de bienestar* exist in most communities; these are elected councils charged with generally maintaining and improving public facilities. These councils may collect fees from itinerant entertainers; they also hold public dances for which they charge admission, and collect fees from people arriving at community fiestas by car. The elections of consejos de bienestar are overseen by the municipio presidents, but for the most part these groups act independently of the cabecera. The *Padres de Familia*, consisting of all parents with schoolchildren, is organized and administered in each community by the schoolteachers. This group makes decisions on school matters and may tax itself for improvement of school grounds and buildings.

Aside from these entities, the communities have no political structure except for that of the ejidos. Ejidos are land-grant communities organized by the federal government. Each family has a plot, which cannot be sold and can only be inherited by one person. Each ejido member has a vote at ejido meetings. There are six elected officials in every ejido: the president, secretary, and treasurer, and a three-member "vigilance committee" charged with making sure that the other three do not misuse ejido funds. In addition to the elected officers, most ejidos have several *sociedades de crédito*, organized in order to obtain credit from the Rural Bank. The bank prefers to work with large groups for the sake of efficiency and to keep paperwork down. Because most ejidos have several sociedades de crédito, ejidatarios may choose the sociedad they feel is most effective and honest. Most ejidos also have a few maverick members who do not trust the bank and make credit arrangements with private individuals. These arrangements usually feature much higher interest rates than the bank's, but because of the personal relationship between borrower and lender, the borrower often feels that there is less chance of being cheated.

The southern Sonora ejidos are organized into the Asociación de Ejidos del Sur de Sonora (ASESS), which, in turn, is affiliated with the peasants' union that makes up a part of the national political party, the Partido Revolucionario Institucional (PRI). ASESS holds meetings where information is exchanged on crop prices, innovations in fertilizers or crops, and government policies affecting ejidos. It is not really a powerful association, although it potentially has lobbying power within the federal government.

The Instituto Nacional Indigenista (INI), a federal agency established to hispanicize Mexico's Indians, has an office in Etchojoa with jurisdiction over the Mayos and Yaquis in Sonora. This agency has established five boarding-schools for Mayo-speaking children, and has a scholarship program for those seeking to continue their education beyond the first six years guaranteed by the federal government. The INI hires *promotores*, community-development agents who speak Mayo, to ascertain community problems and possible solutions for them in the hamlets where Mayos live.

result of these historical and ecological factors, over 50% of the population in this area is monolingual Spanish-speaking Mestizo (INI 1976), and the region is more sparsely populated. There are no tiny Mayo private plots such as those along the river, and the ejido plots--some owned by descendants of Mayos--are larger.

In many of the rural communities here, there is a sense of rawness not found in the much older villages and hamlets along the river; there is also a greater feeling among the inhabitants that change, progress, is possible for them. This is probably a correct view. Because their land yields a viable income, most of these ejidatarios do not have to work as jornaleros; in fact, some must hire workers at peak work periods. Many of those jornaleros come from the lower Mayo, although by no means all of the residents of the northern region have land rights. The wealthier ejidatarios can send their children to school, and some even to secondary and trade schools, because they can afford the tuition and do not require the children's labor on the farm. The sense of upward mobility is much greater than in the lower Mayo, where survival is the major goal.

A still different set of circumstances prevails to the south of the river. About 15 kilometers southwest of Huatabampo, the irrigation district ends and the landscape reverts to thorn forest. It is probably not a coincidence that here are found several comunidades indígenas, special entities established by the federal government to protect the land and other legal rights of traditional Indian groups. Comunidad means "community", and probably originally referred to landholding patterns in these entities rather than to their settlement patterns. The land is held in common by the *comuneros*. This means that all comuneros have the right to run livestock, and all may farm any quantity of land. The general poverty of the comunidades for the most part prevents misuse of these rights, although non-comuneros often attempt to run cattle on comunidad property. The lack of water makes it impossible for any one comunero to use land coveted by others. At the same time, each comunero knows exactly how many hectares of land he or she has a right to farm if by some miracle water were made available. There has recently been some attempt to limit the number of head of livestock allowed to each comunero, but no formal rules have been made in any of the comunidades. Although comuneros are proud of their comunidad membership and jealously guard their rights, most of them survive only by working as jornaleros in the irrigated region.

If the irrigation system brought with it other elements of development, these are lacking outside the area it reaches. Within the district, paved roads provide access to many of the communities, although most of the smaller hamlets are still reached only by dirt paths. Similarly, all of the villages and larger hamlets have running water, although this generally takes the form of one tap per household and does not include such amenities as indoor plumbing. Even these signs of development are for the most part absent in the comunidades. With the exception of the international highway, which transects the comunidad region, this area has no paved roads. The large village of Masiaca has running water, and some of the larger surrounding hamlets boast communal water-taps, but in general, water for household consumption is obtained from wells, carried from small streams, or bought from traveling water-sellers who transport their cargo by mule-cart. The per capita number of schools and clinics is also much smaller in the comunidades than in the irrigation district.

Each comunidad has a president, secretary, and treasurer, who maintain census records and hold infrequent meetings when decisions must be made by the comunidad as a whole. Ideally, the president seeks federal aid for comunidad improvement and organizes work parties for such projects as road maintenance. In fact, little actual work is done either by the elected officials, who are not paid, or by the comunidad as a whole. There is a sense of membership in a corporate body, but in daily life there is little cause to refer to the comunidad.

The paucity of water and other government-sponsored services makes for a very sparse and scattered population in this region. The comuneros live in the aboriginal Mayo settlement pattern of scattered hamlets, most of which consist of one or more extended families. Each nuclear family has its own household, but households tend to cluster in groups in which the males are related. A few comuneros attempt to farm small plots with the aid of small dams during the rainy summer months, but the majority use their comunidad rights mainly for grazing their goats and a few cattle.

The term indígena, like the term comunidad, is somewhat inaccurate in reference to these entities. It is true that most comuneros are unarguably Mayo, but there are some who are Mestizo in their own and others' estimation. How they came to be comuneros is accounted for in various ways. Some claim Mayo ancestry, and some are said to have been given comunero status in the years of turmoil following the Revolution. Still others have been accused by Mayo comuneros of obtaining land rights through force or trickery. Many of these Mestizos, when questioned about how they came to be comuneros, dismiss the term "indígena" as an invention of the government and irrelevant to the realities of the situation. In the past, comunidad government has often been controlled by the wealthier minority, considered Mestizo by their opponents. The issue of ethnic identity and land rights has been controversial in the comunidades to an extent not found in ejidos and other communities, precisely because "indígena" has different meanings to different people.

The Occupational Structure

Most rural residents of the Mayo region are employed directly in agriculture. However, many practice other occupations for a part of the year. Notable among these is fishing. The fishing season lasts from the end of September until the end of May, and fishing rights are rigidly controlled by the government. In all three areas there are part-time fishermen, and near the sea there are some who fish full-time . Fishing is usually done in cooperatives established by the federal government, although some private boat-owners hire workers to man the boats and bring in the fish, which the owners then market. In this situation, the employees earn a percentage of the catch. In recent years the INI has worked to develop a fishing cooperative among the younger male members of three comunidades indígenas. This effort has had mixed results, stemming from the inexperience of the comuneros in both fishing and business techniques.

Apart from fishing, there are several other part-time occupations. In the comunidades, there is substantial dependence on proceeds from the sale of wood cut in the thorn forest; this wood is used for fuel and often as fencing. Another source of revenue for comuneros is the sale of medicinal herbs, which grow wild in the thorn forest and are still used extensively by many residents of the valley and beyond.

Curanderos, or curers, who use these herbs and other means of alleviating illness are also to be found in the Mayo region. They are consulted before, after, and often simultaneously with regular medical doctors. The powers of the curanderos, like the powers of the saints, are believed to overlap with modern medicine; they are not seen as mutually exclusive.

Although there is no heavy industry in either Huatabampo or Navojoa, a substantial amount of service and agriculturally related employment is available to forward-looking young people. There are several packinghouses in both Huatabampo and Navojoa for the processing of U.S.-bound vegetables grown in the region. These provide jobs mostly for residents of the towns, but there are some rural employees also. For the most part, town jobs are held by those toward the Mestizo end of the cultural spectrum.

Conclusion: Ecology and Economy in Southern Sonora

The Mayo area represents a very small part of Mexico's agricultural land. Compared to the Yaqui area, it is much smaller and much less productive. At the same time, anyone who visits the region can see that it is economically developed. The large, well-tended fields, the numerous farm machines, and the modern towns bespeak a prosperity unseen in most developing nations. Even in this small corner of the world, however, there are economic and historical factors that make for discrepancies in the effects of that development. Here is to be found in stark reality the inequality brought about by development: in terms of the trickle-down theory, the trickle stops at the borders of the irrigation district, and its force varies within these borders.

The disparities in the social and economic structures of the region make for wide variations in the ways in which individual families live their lives, see their future, and account for their actions. In attempting to understand one aspect of these lives--ethnic identity--it is necessary to examine how external constraints affect ethnic expression in given circumstances. These circumstances vary most obviously among the three zones of the valley that have been created by a combination of historical and ecological factors. In the nonirrigated zone are to be found the fewest of these opportunities and, consequently, the communities least changed by development. The densely populated region near the river, while obviously changed radically, still provides fewer opportunities to its rural residents than the more sparsely populated region to the north. Here, ejidos have enough land and enough technical inputs to have created real, permanent economic gains for their members. Because of this microenvironmental variation within the valley, a closer inspection of specific communities in these regions is necessary to a fuller understanding of ethnic change and continuity in the valley as a whole.

5

Júpare: Village on the Lower Mayo

q: Are there yoremes who speak Mayo but pretend not to so people will think they are yoris?

a: That's right.

q: Here in Júpare?

a: There are some. Although they are yoremes they don't want to speak Mayo because they don't want to be yoremes, they want to appear yori. As if they were ashamed to be yoremes. For example, if I were a person like this and I saw some people in a group, and they were yoris, and a person arrived and started speaking Mayo with me, I would answer in Spanish because those yoris were there and I would want them to think better of me. People like that want to be yoris. But if I myself am with some people who call themselves yoris, and someone arrives and speaks to me in Mayo, I answer him in Mayo....I am not ashamed of what I am.

(interview with a resident of Júpare)

Introduction

Some 5 kilometers southwest of Huatabampo and 1 kilometer from the Mayo river is the village of Júpare (population: 2500). It was in this region that the densest aboriginal population of Mayos was found, although Júpare's residents today include people from all along the cultural continuum. History has not recorded the founding of Júpare, but the oral tradition of the village holds that it was moved there from Pueblo Viejo, the site of the historic town of Santa Cruz. Indeed, many of the residents of Júpare claim to be originally from Pueblo Viejo. It would appear that the removal from Santa Cruz took place at some time after the Mayos surrendered to Mexico in 1888 and before the 1910 Revolution. Júpare was not one of the original Mayo pueblos, but its religious ceremonies are today more popular, more numerous, and more elaborate than those of any other village.

Whatever the date and circumstances of its founding, Júpare was certainly an entity in 1913 when the last Mayo uprising occurred under the leadership of Miguel Totoliguoqui. The Mayos massed northwest of the river and attacked Pueblo Viejo and Júpare, killing the Mestizo leaders and destroying their possessions. Many Mestizos took flight to the sierra, returning only after Totoliguoqui was captured and killed by Mestizo soldiers at El Citavaro, 6 kilometers northeast of Júpare.

Although economic and political demands motivated the Totoliguoqui uprising, it manifested along ethnic lines. Despite the general pervasiveness of a cultural continuum in everyday matters, this ethnic conflict is still remembered today, kept alive by frequent retelling of the story from both Mestizo and Mayo points of view. Informants are slow to point a finger at specific village residents as descendants of participants in the uprising, but the knowledge that it occurred, and was ethnic in nature, continues in the minds of Jupareños.

Ethnic conflict did not end in 1913. The eruption of violence in the 1930s is another subject of frequent stories in Júpare and the surrounding hamlets. Under the anticlerical administration of Governor Calles (1930-36), the Catholic Church was for a time outlawed. In Júpare and several other villages, Mestizos took advantage of this anticlerical campaign to burn the Mayo saints and destroy their churches. No one was ever punished for this destruction of property. The Mayos were allowed to rebuild their churches within ten years after the burning of the saints. This event is nevertheless still a sore point for those at the Mayo end of the spectrum. It has also helped make the Mayos' religious system an important aspect of their ethnic identity; and religion as a basis for political action is still feared by the Mestizos, although the fear at this point is perhaps unjustified.

Ethnic Mixing

Ethnic conflict has been important in Júpare's history, but it has not been the only kind of interaction between Mayos and Mestizos. Several important institutions in the village ignore ethnicity and facilitate smoothing over the underlying ethnic differences. Perhaps the most important of these institutions is the ejido, established in 1934. Ejido membership is not based on ethnic identity, and Júpare's ejidatarios typify the cultural continuum to be found in the village and in the region in general. Ejido meetings, however, are conducted in Spanish. The ejido leaders consider themselves Mestizo and are so considered by others. More than one ejidatario explained to me that the officers are selected for their ability to deal with bank agents, and the most adept at this are the Mestizos--it is assumed that their allegiance will be to the ejido rather than to Mestizos as such.

The ideal of the ejido system is that all families in the village have ejido rights and that all ejidatarios live in the village, but this is seldom the reality. Only 17% of the households surveyed in Júpare had ejidatarios, and many ejido members live in hamlets near their fields. The ejido, then, is an entity that transcends ethnic identity but does not include the community as a whole.

Júpare's school, on the other hand, is more inclusive. Although rural areas in general have few schools, Júpare has a complete elementary school. Most children attend for at least three years, and parents try to keep their children in school as long as possible. Children from all households attend the school; many Spanish-speakers learn a few words of Mayo in the schoolyard, and it is rare today in Júpare for a school-age Mayo child not to know Spanish.

The Padres de Familia, an organization of the parents of schoolchildren, includes most of Júpare's adults. This group wields little power, its jurisdiction being merely over school matters, but it is significant in that it does not reinforce ethnic distinctions. As with the ejido, the leadership is Mestizo and the meetings are conducted in Spanish.

Júpare also boasts a government medical clinic. Ethnic identity does not determine who may be treated. The clinic is thus available to all regardless of ethnicity or income. Unlike many rural people in other parts of Mexico, Jupareños do not distrust modern medicine; people throughout the cultural continuum consult both doctors and curanderos, often simultaneously, and in conjunction with making vows to saints.

Another factor that contributes to ethnic mixing is occupation. Although Mestizos more than Mayos work at high-paying skilled-labor jobs such as tractor driver or foreman, the majority on both sides of the cultural continuum are either jornaleros or ejidatarios (see Table 1). There is also no significant difference in years of education for heads of households: almost all have had less than two years of schooling. These aspects of daily life do not provide any means of ethnic distinction by occupation or educational achievement. When ethnic traits and income levels are compiled into indices, there is a similar lack of correlation (see Table 2).

TABLE 1: Ethnic Identity and Occupation of Heads of Households in Júpare

Ethnic Continuum

	Mestizo				Mayo
	0	1	2	3	4
Jornalero	4	7	4	9	8
Ejidatario	1	0	4	1	1
Skilled	1	3	2	0	0

n=45

Note: Ethnic traits are: Mayo surname, knowledge of the Mayo language, having a house cross throughout the year, and being a major participant in the Mayo religious system. Individuals having all four traits are given a score of 4; those with none of these traits receive a score of 0.

TABLE 2: Ethnic Identity of Heads of Households and Income by Household in Júpare

Ethnic Continuum

	Mestizo				Mayo
	0	1	2	3	4
Low income	2	5	6	7	7
Middle income	4	3	4	1	1
High income	1	0	0	0	0

n=41

Note: Income for each household is based on the number of workers, their occupations, and the amount of land and livestock controlled. Low income is $1000 U.S. or less in 1978 dollars, middle income is $1050-$3,000, and high income is $3050-$7500 yearly. Ethnic continuum is based on the ethnic traits listed in note in Table 1.

Ethnic Cleavage

Although certain political entities in the village downplay ethnic distinctions, others help to promote them. Two of these institutions are the delegado de policia and the consejo de bienestar. The deputy of police is appointed by the president of the Huatabampo municipio. He is invariably at the Mestizo end of the cultural continuum, and to an extent represents Mestizo interests in keeping order, especially at fiestas. The council, also clearly Mestizo, is in charge of raising money for improvements in the community. This group, like the delegado, is sometimes seen as representing Mestizo interests in such activities as building the dance hall and maintaining streets. The consejo de bienestar holds secular dances, can levy small taxes, and charges fees from itinerant entertainments such as open-air movie shows and carnivals. The council also collects a fee from every car entering the village during the major Júpare fiesta; this illustrates how intertwined are the secular and religious aspects of the fiesta.

In counterbalance to the consejo de bienestar is the church consejo. Both these groups are elected by the village, and both handle substantial amounts of money. Members of the church consejo, however, are at the Mayo extreme of the cultural continuum, but versed enough in Mestizo culture to be able to read, write, and keep accounts. Their responsibility is limited to the church building and the fiesta ramada and kitchens. Income for the maintenance of these comes from contributions to the saints from the faithful; in Júpare this income can be as much as $1000 U.S. per annum, a comparatively enormous amount.

Although statistically there is not a significant relationship between ethnic identity and occupation, there are certain jobs that only Mayo speakers may hold. Teachers in the schools set up by the Instituto Nacional Indigenista must pass a test showing fluency in Mayo; this is also true of community-development agents hired by the INI to attempt to hispanicize Mayos and bring them into the national society. At the same time, many jobs require skills and special knowledge that are available only to those who can afford special training. In Júpare, these are undeniably at the Mestizo end of the cultural continuum. Likewise, the only people who own over 10 hectares of land in the village are at the Mestizo extreme of the spectrum.

In summary, ethnically homogeneous organizations and a small number of specialized occupations tend to continue the pattern of ethnic cleavage established by historical conflicts in Júpare. However, there are several institutions that ignore ethnic identity and have a centripetal effect on the village population. The ejido, school, and clinic help make ethnic conflict between Mayos and Mestizos too costly in social and economic terms to be worthwhile for either side.

Júpare: Village on the Lower Mayo

Situational Ethnicity

We may speak of structures and entities in Júpare, but the truth is that these manifest only in situations--meetings, conversations, fiestas, and so on--which involve individuals who represent a complex of possible behaviors elicited by those situations. The personal histories of the people involved, the history of the entity, and the goals and motivations of each individual, all contribute to the overall form of the event.

Meetings of the consejo de bienestar, for example, are only attended by those toward the Mestizo side of the cultural continuum, because the consejo is seen as representing Mestizo interests. This situation elicits Mestizo behavior by default. The meetings are carried on entirely in Spanish. The members of the consejo strive to demonstrate their knowledge of such Mestizo qualities as the ability to read and write, and an understanding of the political activities of Huatabampo, upon which much of the welfare of Júpare depends. If the subject of the meeting is how to raise money, consejo members propose such actions as secular dances or raffles. Individual members compete to get their pet programs implemented: to know of a good band, or be able to get at reduced cost an appliance suitable for raffling, are important ways of gaining prestige not only at council meetings but in the community as a whole. These kinds of knowledge demonstrate, on one hand, a certain amount of familiarity with the world beyond Júpare, a familiarity that most Mestizos covet.

On the other hand, activities in and around the church on Sunday mornings feature situations that generally elicit Mayo behavior. The church consejo meets on the porch at the side of the church on most Sundays. Although the meeting is public, it is conducted entirely in Mayo, and onlookers are not invited to participate. Sunday is also when the fiesteros perform a ceremony with the Júpare flag inside the church. This event is followed by a recitation of the Rosary, led by the maestro. The fiesteros then retire to a special ramada behind the church, where they and the maestro eat.

Only individuals directly involved with Mayo religious activities are found at the church at this time; the required language is Mayo, and approval accrues to those who clearly understand what is going on. People who betray ignorance of the meaning of the ceremonies are ridiculed by the more knowledgeable, and inability to speak Mayo is scorned. The proceedings are rather complex, and in order to behave correctly one must have a significant amount of knowledge about tradition, ritual meaning, and the structure of the ceremonial system. In order for this system to continue, the sanctions against ignorance must be rather strong. The Sunday morning ceremonies provide weekly situations in which Mayo ethnic identity is strongly reinforced; it is in part because of these weekly ceremonies and their characteristic overt sanctions against non-Mayo behavior that the system, and Mayo culture, continue to exist in Júpare.

It might be argued that the number of people involved in extreme Mayo or Mestizo situations at any time is so small as to be unimportant in terms of overall village life. For example, the total number of people in and around the church on Sunday never exceeds 30, and often features as few as 15. The consejo de bienestar is made up of 5 people and its meetings never include more than 10 individuals. The decisions of both consejos affect many more people, however, and thus behavior at the meetings is important because of the power of their members. Furthermore, fiesteros change every year; many people are involved in the long run. Finally, the two consejos and the fiesteros bring about the fiestas, and are responsible for their success. This success is defined in economic terms for the consejo de bienestar and in ceremonial terms by the church consejo and the religious leaders. Both economic and religious success for the fiestas depend on a large attendance; thus, although the number of organizers is small, they assure the existence of large fiestas, which in turn serve both to demonstrate and to continue the system of ethnicity.

The consejo de bienestar and the church consejo meetings are examples of extreme situations eliciting exclusively either Mestizo or Mayo behavioral traits. These are the only relatively public situations where ethnic slurs are sometimes heard. Situations in which extreme ethnic behavior is clearly not wanted are those involving representatives of the entire cultural continuum. These contexts include daily interactions in village stores and in the school and clinic, visiting among neighbors, and most work scenes. In all these situations, Mayo and Spanish are intermixed and there is little pressure to appear either Mayo or Mestizo. Individuals behave in the way most comfortable to them.

The fiestas are probably the most ethnically complex situations found in Júpare. They are undeniably the most popular. Only the major fiesta of the Santísima Trinidad (Holy Trinity) features a secular carnival, but all the fiestas coincide with secular dances at the community dance floor. Music from the dance is frequently heard even inside the church and certainly in the ramada where the traditional deer and pascola dances are held. At the same time, the religious processions are public, and the fireworks signaling various periods of the religious fiesta are heard throughout the village. People drift back and forth from secular to religious situations depending on what is happening in each.

To the casual observer, it may appear that the people at the extremes of the cultural continuum remain in their respective ethnic contexts during the fiesta--the "most Mayo" staying near the church and ramada, and the "most Mestizo" attending only the dance. However, even actual fiesta participants (fiesteros, matachines, etc.) make their way to the dance or the carnival rides if they can afford the price of admission. Similarly, those at the Mestizo end of the cultural spectrum feel that the church is theirs, too, and most believe in the saints if not in the Mayo ways of honoring them. The religious dancers likewise have universal appeal. Mestizos are therefore found in the church and the dance ramada during the fiesta.

An individual's behavior at the fiesta can oscillate during one 12-hour period. For example, a young man from the center of the cultural continuum may begin the main fiesta day with such evidence of religious devotion as bringing a candle to the saint and marching in the procession to meet the visiting saint from another village. In the afternoon, he may (if invited) eat at the kitchen ramada and later watch the deer and pascola dancers, making ribald jokes along with them in Mayo and drinking mescal with other fiesta-goers. In the evening, after donning his best clothes, he might go to the secular dance or, if he does not have the price of admission, he may stand outside the walled dance floor, called the *cancha*, drinking beer and talking to other men in Spanish. When the evening prayers begin in the church, he might attend them and then return to the dance ramada for the rest of the evening. Extreme Mestizos would of course be unable to converse in Mayo, and would probably not be invited to eat at the fiesta kitchens.

Women are somewhat more restricted, and must travel in groups. Fewer women than men are found in the ramada, and more women than men are found in the church. Women never drink in public, and only men stand in knots outside the dance cancha. Women are admitted free of charge to the secular dance, and as long as they are accompanied by other women, or by their husbands or children, they come and go as they please.

Individual behavior varies, but the situations at the fiestas remain rather stable. This reveals a certain amount of agreement about the nature of these contexts and the way people should act in each of them. Nor are these models for behavior unconscious; when asked about them, informants agree that the dance ramada demands Mayo behavior and the cancha is more of a Mestizo situation.

The dance ramada and the fiesta kitchens are definitely Mayo: Mayo is the dominant language, and people well-versed in Mayo traditions are clearly in charge. At the same time, the dance cancha and the carnival rides are clearly Mestizo. The church is not so well-defined during the fiesta as on Sunday mornings, however. Individual behavior coincides more with the actor's position on the cultural continuum: people from the Mestizo end will bring flowers or donate money, but will never be fiesteros or matachines. These roles are generally filled by people on the Mayo side, but not necessarily at the extreme. Individuals who put on hábitos tend to be from the middle of the continuum: neither extremely Mayo nor extremely Mestizo.

Ethnic Change

Despite the fact that ethnic expression is determined situationally in many cases, most individuals think of themselves as either Mayo or Mestizo. There is some ambivalence among families in the middle of the cultural continuum in Júpare, but for the most part people are willing to declare themselves on one side or the other: in the household survey, there is a high correlation between objective ethnic traits and declared ethnic identity. There is also a category of people who "want to be yoris." These people are looked down on by those who definitely do not want to be yoris, but they are tolerated by the Mestizos themselves. There are definite ways of announcing this desire to change ethnic identity, and the process of change is also defined in public, often in religious situations.

One of the more obvious ways to change ethnic identity is to deny knowing how to speak Mayo. This is not possible in a village the size of Júpare, where everyone knows who speaks Mayo and who does not. The next-best solution is simply to cease speaking Mayo, answering Mayo with Spanish. This is a simple procedure, because everyone understands Spanish. Because it is so easy, language-use change can be quite rapid.

There are other, more subtle ways of changing ethnic identity, and these are always associated with insistence on Spanish in conversation. One way to announce the change is to attend Wednesday Mass in the church. Every Wednesday the priest from Huatabampo says Mass in the Júpare church. The church consejo, or at least the president, must be on hand to open the church, but the people who attend the Mass are for the most part from the Mestizo side of the spectrum. By attending this Mass, individuals who are considered Mayo by others initiate the change to the Mestizo side. The congregation at Mass is almost exclusively female, but the woman who goes to Mass speaks for her entire family in making the change.

Another context in which ethnic change can occur is during the fiesta of the Virgin of Guadalupe. This is a nine-day festival that features velaciones similar in some ways to the Lenten velaciones. These, however, are conducted by the same people who attend Wednesday Mass, and their content is somewhat different from the Lenten vigils. Although the prayers are conducted by the Mayo maestro, they are all in Spanish and quite orthodox. There are no fireworks, no masked dancers, and no cocoon-rattles in evidence. As with the Lenten vigils, it is mostly women who do the praying; unlike those, however, there are no men drinking and joking on the sidelines. The Guadalupe velaciones, in short, are sedate. The food served is emulative of the Mexican middle class: sandwiches, salads, cakes, and the like. *Guacabaqui*, the traditional beef soup served at Mayo fiestas, is definitely not served.

Sponsors of the Guadalupe vigils vie with each other over who has the calmest, best-attended velación. This is also an opportunity to display personal possessions and a Mestizo lifestyle consciously copied from television and from Huatabampo residents. For a family that wants to become Mestizo, a Guadalupe velación is an excellent way to demonstrate just how Mestizo they have become: plastic armchairs, a television set, a cement floor, and kitchen appliances are examples of Mestizo status symbols.

At the same time that these Mestizo velaciones are going on, there is a Mayo fiesta of the traditional sort. This fiesta does not overlap completely with the velaciones, for they go on every night of the festival, while the fiesta is only on the last two nights. On these nights, there is a clear difference between the two ceremonies, which are held simultaneously but in different places. The Guadalupe festival is important because it forces a choice between ethnically defined situations, both of them religious.

On the last night of the fiesta, the Mestizos have a procession through the village, featuring a truck carrying the decorated picture of the Virgin, followed by children dressed in white. This procession ends at the church, where a mixture of Mayo and Mestizo rituals takes place, conducted by the maestro. This event tends to smooth over the more obvious differences between the groups involved; the fact that the Virgin of Guadalupe is the patron saint of Mexico, and that all Jupareños are Mexicans, is brought out in the songs and prayers. After the ceremony, the Mestizos go home and the Mayo fiesta continues in the usual way, ending the following day.

The Wednesday Mass and the Guadalupe festival provide contexts for announcing and verifying ethnic change, but they are not excessively disturbing contexts in that they do not involve issues over which people might clash, such as jobs or educational opportunities. They thus provide ways in which people can change their ethnicity without a great deal of conflict within the village. Given this rather easy means of becoming Mestizo, the problem is to explain why everyone does not. If there is little economic motivation for remaining Mayo, and a certain amount of prestige in being Mestizo, why are there still discernible Mayos?

In many ways, being Mayo has its own satisfactions, while changing to Mestizo takes energy and risks ostracism by friends and relatives. In Júpare, kin are important in defining many aspects of an individual's and even a family's life. Unless an entire kin group is willing and able to make the change, the single family must expect to be rejected by the rest of the kin group, at least to some extent. The negative sanctions against change must be slighter than the advantages of changing. Usually, this means that there must be economic reasons for changing. If a family has somehow managed to increase its income, it will probably want to be separated from its poorer relatives in any event. Becoming Mestizo makes this easier, and eliminates the necessity to help relatives with fiesta costs. In fact, a refusal to donate time or money to a relative's fiesta almost always elicits an accusation that the shirker "wants to be a yori." In order to understand why everyone has not become Mestizo in Júpare, it is necessary to examine the opportunities for economic and social mobility in the village.

Social and Economic Opportunities

Júpare in many ways epitomizes the boom and bust of the post-revolutionary era in Mexico. With the implementation of the irrigation system came the establishment of the ejido and the opening up of employment opportunities on private farms. The shift to mechanized farming made possible specializations such as tractor driver and combine operator. Development brought with it the six-grade school, the government clinic, and running water and electricity for every household in the village. The school represents an opportunity for social mobility for all villagers: jobs which require a certificate of six years of education are now available to Jupareños, although not in the village itself.

With the economic slowdown that began in 1970, many opportunities and services became frozen. The sons of ejidatarios cannot expect new land to be opened to them, and the number of available jornalero jobs has not increased with the number of workers. Some Júpare young men are members of the new collective ejidos established by Echeverría in 1976, but they are a very small percentage of those seeking land or work. The result is systematic underemployment. The proximity of Júpare to Huatabampo makes it possible for Jupareños to get work there, and this eases the situation somewhat, but it also exposes them daily to the extremes of wealth so blatant in the town. The great social mobility that gave the wealthy the position they now enjoy is no longer to be hoped for by anyone in southern Sonora, and Júpare residents working in Huatabampo must face this fact every day.

The same situation holds true for government services: although many more elementary-school graduates would go on to secondary school if there were one in Júpare, there is little hope of the government's building one. Some students go to secondary school in Huatabampo, but the vast majority merely swell the ranks of the underemployed. Services such as agrarian-reform agents and agricultural-extension agents have also been curtailed, and although these do not directly affect the lives of many Júpare residents, they affect the overall quality of life in the village.

There can be little doubt that the economic boom in Sonora affected Mestizos more than Mayos, in general. This is also the case in Júpare: people who spoke Spanish and had political ties with Huatabampo and the cities were certain to benefit more than Mayos, although many Mestizos were little more prepared for development than the Mayos. The fact that being Mestizo is associated with being wealthy means that those Mayos who sought wealth automatically sought Mestizo status. Had growth been perpetual, it seems likely that today there would be few Mayos in Júpare, given the pattern of ethnic change found in the village among those few who do prosper. At the very least, Mayo ethnicity, like that of Buaysiacobe, would be less linked to the traditional culture. However, with the closing of many opportunities and the increasing population density in the lower river region, the motivations to change ethnic identity have also declined.

In the face of great Mestizo wealth in Huatabampo and the hopelessness of ever sharing it, Mayos in Júpare have in some ways intensified their interest in the fiestas: there are more fiestas in Júpare than in other villages, and fiesta expenses are greater here. Júpare has four fiestas

Júpare: Village on the Lower Mayo

over and above Easter, while Masiaca, for example, has only two. The total yearly expenditure for a Júpare fiestero ranges from $200 to $400 U.S. Masiaca fiesta costs range from $50 to $200 U.S. It was among people from the hamlets around Júpare that the most recent millenarian movement (N.Ross Crumrine 1977; O'Connor 1979) flourished. This movement featured fiestas similar in some ways to the traditional fiestas, but with some new traits such as special prayers and handshakes. Participants believed that only those who performed these special rituals and returned to the old Mayo ways would be saved from destruction in the form of a flood. This type of social movement fits Aberle's (1966:330) category of transformative movements, which "seem to appeal to people who have been. . .extruded from their niche. . . into more marginal niches, and who cannot foresee another niche which offers reasonable security."

Conclusion

The nature of ethnic identity in Júpare is complex. A history of ethnic conflict, the presence of long-time Mestizo residents, and the existence of ethnically defined institutions make for a certain amount of opposition between the two extremes of the cultural continuum. This cleavage is mitigated somewhat by institutions that are not defined ethnically. Moreover, most occupations are not defined ethnically, although those that are tend to point up the economic marginality suffered by those at the Mayo extreme of the continuum.

Throughout the Mayo region, ethnic expression is often determined by the social situation in which it takes place. In Júpare, there are situations that elicit Mestizo behavior and those that demand Mayo behavior. The most complex and most widely attended public events are the fiestas; these elicit both kinds of behavior at different times and places.

To speak of situations as eliciting or determining behavior might seem to give them some mysterious power of their own. In reality, situations themselves represent agreements among the individuals involved about the correct behavior for a given context. These agreements in turn are based on past situations, on instruction or example from elders and kin, and on frequent or special conversations about the correct way to behave. This does not imply that at the secular dance, for example, people formally discuss how to dance or whether to speak Spanish. Normal human interaction is, of course, largely informal and often based on intuition.

If individuals behave in ways elicited by given situations, they may also take advantage of situations to make statements about themselves and their families; here is the opportunity to change status within the community. In Júpare, the major kind of change is in ethnic identity. It is possible for families to announce a desire to change their identity by attending specific events. Despite the ease of this change, it is not occurring at the rate one might expect, given the prestige system of the region. The primary motivation to become Mestizo has always been economic, with obvious social overtones. Development in the lower valley has not kept up with population growth; this means that economic and social opportunities that would encourage ethnic change in Júpare are fewer than they were in the boom period of the 1950s and 1960s.

This relative deprivation, rather than merely slowing the rate of change, has to some extent created a greater emphasis on fiesta participation and on participation in a short-lived but popular millenarian movement. The village's history of ethnic cleavage of course explains part of this continued ethnic opposition; given a slowdown in economic growth, Mayos will always see themselves as deprived of progress by Mestizos, at least in Júpare. This deprivation has resulted in an intensification of the religious system that defines Mayo identity and emphasizes the differences created by economic marginalization.

6

Buaysiacobe, a New Community

q: Would you say that you are better off now than before?

a (1): I remember, around 1952, when we saw the canals they were making in the thorn forest, we thought that that land would never be able to be cultivated, because we didn't know or understand what would happen to our ejido. We thought the people who were building the canals were crazy. We didn't know they were building a dam. And now the valley is very beautiful. Now we have more than 5,000 hectares under cultivation.

a (2): The people, although they don't understand, they are waking up. In a general assembly, everyone speaks up, although inarticulately. They say, that's not the way things should be.

(interview with two members of the Buaysiacobe ejido)

Introduction

Although only 25 kilometers north of Júpare and about the same size, Buaysiacobe (population: 2,000) differs from that community in important ways. In Buaysiacobe, ethnic homogeneity and the availability of substantial economic opportunities for all members of the community combine to produce a very different set of circumstances. In Júpare, economic change is expressed and interpreted as ethnic change because of the few opportunities for economic advancement and the underlying ethnic cleavage in the village. The different circumstances in Buaysiacobe lead to the downplaying of ethnicity, especially in the context of economic change.

Buaysiacobe was established in 1939 as a collective ejido. There were a few houses at the site before that time, but the community as it is today essentially dates from the beginning of the ejido. The village was laid out in equal plots, and each ejidatario family was given a plot on which to build a house. Each family also received 20 hectares of uncleared thorn forest, which at that time had no access to irrigation water. Buaysiacobe as a community is quite new, but many of the ejidatarios came from nearby; over half of the heads of households in my survey were born within 7.5 kilometers of the village. The majority of Buaysiacobe residents are also self-declared Mayos, although many of them admit that others might consider them Mestizos. Rural Bank agents call Buaysiacobe "muy civilizado" (very civilized) in comparison with other Indian villages, such as Júpare.

The fact that its members came from the area and are mostly of Mayo ancestry distinguishes it from other ejidos in the region northwest of the Mayo river. Many of these are made up of people who came from southern Mexico to take advantage of the new land-grants; therefore, many of these communities are mostly Mestizo. Buaysiacobe is an interesting case because it is a village of Indians who have been given the same kinds of opportunities generally made available only to Mestizos. It is precisely because of these opportunities that Buaysiacobe Mayos are today considered "muy civilizados."

The "civilizing" process got off to a slow start after 1939. As a collective ejido, Buaysiacobe suffered from all the problems of collective farms. Production was low because ejidatarios could not see the direct relationship between their labor and total output. Management was corrupt, and the ejido bank even more so. When Erasmus visited Buaysiacobe in 1958, just after it was converted from a collective to private plots, he found a village of huts where the ejidatarios were disgusted with the bank and the ejido leaders alike. Many ejido plots were rented to Mestizos or worked on reverse sharecropping, where a Mestizo provided seeds and equipment in return for half the crop (Erasmus 1978:78-81). The ejidatarios had only recently received water rights in the Yaqui Irrigation District, and many were still working at the grueling task of clearing their lands.

Buaysiacobe's aspect today presents a startling contrast to the impoverished community described by Erasmus. Large brick houses, some with indoor plumbing, line the main street. Here also are the ejido assembly hall, the six-grade school, and the Social Security clinic. There is even a branch of the Rural Bank adjacent to the ejido office. Kitchen gardens are common in the large household plots, which also afford room for medium-sized livestock such as pigs and goats.

At the beginning of Buaysiacobe's success story lies the large amount of land and water rights provided for each family. There are two reasons for the larger parcels. One is that at the time of the grant there was no water available, and it was assumed that only livestock could be raised. The other reason is that this area was sparsely inhabited in comparison with the lower river region, and there was less competition over land in the first place.

The reasons for economic viability in Buaysiacobe go beyond mere land-ownership; if this were not so, the village would not have been so poor in 1958. The ejido leaders so despised at that time were replaced by leaders who had an interest in making the ejido successful; these leaders now enjoy a considerable amount of prestige in the community and in the regional peasant union. The success of Buaysiacobe is also attributable to the interest of state leaders in making the community a kind of agricultural showplace. The village is held up as an example of a well-run, prosperous ejido. The interest in Buaysiacobe's success extends to Rural Bank officials, who need to have productive farms in order to keep afloat. The large size of each ejido plot makes economic productivity and efficiency more possible than with the much smaller plots of, for example, the Júpare ejido.

Ethnic Homogeneity

Buaysiacobe does not have Júpare's history of ethnic conflict; this is partially because it has little history of any kind. It is also because the majority of residents are of Mayo ancestry: there is little opportunity for ethnic conflict. The ejido leaders are all Mayo-speakers, as are the members of the consejo de bienestar. Although ejido meetings are begun in Spanish, it is not uncommon for ejidatarios to make extended statements in Mayo; because virtually everyone understands Mayo, there is no reason to insist on Spanish. This is true of the meetings of the consejo de bienestar as well. School classes are conducted entirely in Spanish, but in the playground Mayo is sometimes heard. This is evidently less the case now than formerly, however. In the household survey, 67% of the offspring over 15 years old speak Mayo, but only 18% of those under 15 do.

Buaysiacobe residents are quite proud of their Mayo heritage. It was at El Cerro del Bayájorit, a hill near the village site, that Totoliguoqui and his followers gathered in preparation for their 1913 uprising. This fact is pointed out frequently, especially during discussions about how to deal with the bank agents, the ejidatarios' eternal foes. A photograph of Totoliguoqui and his troops, armed with bows and arrows, is displayed in the ejido office, as is the Mexican flag and a photograph of the President. This kind of ethnic pride is not possible in Júpare, where the nature of the cultural continuum makes ethnic expression more complex.

Economic Homogeneity

The majority of Buaysiacobe residents are ejidatarios, and the majority of the ejidatarios live in the village. In this, Buaysiacobe differs not only from Júpare but from most Mexican communities. The reason for this homogeneity is the newness of the village and the fact that it was explicitly as an ejido that it was established. Recently, jornalero families have begun to settle at the northern edge of the town. They had to seek permission from the ejido, however, to do so. The heads of these households generally work on the ejido parcels, so their livelihoods are as dependent on the success of the ejido as are those of the ejidatarios themselves.

This commonality of economic interests makes for a great deal of solidarity among the villagers. Some factionalism is always present in a group of this size, but the absence of clear-cut reasons for conflict makes it uncommon. It also makes group action more successful. Buaysiacobe has had great success in dealing with regional and even national government and bank officials, and ejidatarios can be sure that if they do not get the full amount of money from their crop sales their leaders will take action to settle the problem. In an amazing demonstration of the political influence of the ejido leaders, a national-level representative of the Agrarian Reform Department spent several months resurveying the entire ejido in response to complaints of encroachment by private landowners. This process required an amount of internal organization too great to be possible in an ejido where internal squabbles over land rights and management of funds predominate, such as nearby San Pedro ejido, where bitter in-fighting has rendered the community helpless to defend itself from encroachment by outsiders.

Buaysiacobe, like Júpare, is situated near a larger town, Bacobampo (population: 8000). Bacobampo, however, does not have the wealth that Huatabampo has. It is smaller, and is not a municipio cabecera, nor does it have a market. It does not have any large, imposing houses like the mansions in Huatabampo. Thus, it does not represent to Mayos a level of wealth to which they can never aspire; on the contrary, the people of Buaysiacobe can look with pride at their own houses and compare them favorably with those of Bacobampo. In the city of Navojoa, where many Buaysiacobe residents go for meetings and shopping, there are the kinds of evidence of wealth found in Huatabampo. All the same, the wealth of Buaysiacobe is great enough to make it possible for its inhabitants to aspire at least to a middle-class lifestyle, if not for themselves, then for their children, whom they can afford to educate beyond sixth grade.

Religion and Ethnic Expression

Ethnic and economic homogeneity make for a lack of concern over who is Mayo and who is not in Buaysiacobe. There is no weekly situation such as Júpare's Sunday church service, which demands exclusively Mayo behavior, or which links being Mayo to participating in specifically Mayo religious rituals. Buaysiacobe's place in the religious system as a whole is not nearly so prominent as either Júpare's or Masiaca village's. Buaysiacobe's folk-Catholic structure is a chapel, not a church. As a consequence, this village does not mount the elaborate Lenten and Easter ceremonies, nor do the fiesteros clean the chapel and perform a weekly ceremony. Those who make vows to be fariseos must complete these vows in another community, most commonly in San Pedro. Thus, the opportunity to express Mayo ethnicity as symbolized by religious behavior is much less frequent in Buaysiacobe than in some other villages of its population size.

At the same time, economic mobility is not linked specifically to ethnic change as it is in Júpare. As Júpare's fiesta provides situations that demand different ethnic expressions, Buaysiacobe's fiesta demonstrates the village's lack of ethnic cleavages. In the first place, the religious aspect of the fiesta is much less important than in Júpare: there are only 6 fiesteros, and they serve for one year only. The church is much smaller than Júpare's, and is not visited by as many people during the fiesta. The secular games and dance are also less impressive than Júpare's, and they are not as distinct ethnically. The fact that most adults speak and understand Mayo means that Mayo is often heard at the dance and games. The entire affair lacks the overtone of ethnic boundaries evident to the knowledgeable observer of the Júpare fiesta.

Another indication of ethnic homogeneity is the fact that the paid performers are not paid by the fiesteros, as they are in every other village where fiestas are held. This cost is covered by the consejo de bienestar, out of community funds. It is true that many of these funds come from fees charged to cars arriving at the fiesta, but the Júpare consejo also charges these fees, and does not use them to cover fiesta costs. The Buaysiacobe fiesta has more dancers than most Júpare fiestas. The dancers are an important attraction at the fiesta, and the willingness of the community as a whole to pay for them clearly demonstrates that the village, and the fiesta, are Mayo.

That the secular consejo de bienestar covers some of the fiesta costs also suggests a trend toward secularization of the fiesta. In Buaysiacobe, the dancers have a much more central role than at Júpare or Masiaca. The explicitly religious aspects of the fiesta, by comparison, are much downplayed: there is no meeting with a saint from another community, no procession around the church or through the village, and only minimal praying within the church.

This secular aspect of Buaysiacobe life is evident in other ways. The use of house crosses is an example. In Buaysiacobe, only 1 of 35 self-declared Mayo households had a house cross all year; this compares with 13 of 22 in Júpare, and 18 of 32 in the Masiaca hamlets. The absence of a Sunday service in Buaysiacobe, as well as the lack of interest in the village on the part of the Catholic priest in nearby Bacobampo, are further indications of a general secularization.

The number of religious vows made by individual Mayos also demonstrates the extent of their commitment to traditional religion. In Buaysiacobe, the number of vows made for heads of households and their spouses does not differ significantly from those in Júpare and the Masiaca hamlets. The number of vows made for their children shows a marked decline in Buaysiacobe, however: only 10% of the households had children with major vows, in contrast to 26% of the Júpare households and 30% of the Masiaca households. This evidence points to a trend away from making vows, and suggests that this trend has been recent.

The separation of religion and ethnic identity expressed in these secular trends accounts in part for the relatively large number of Protestants living in Buaysiacobe. There are three fundamentalist Protestant sects in the village. Attendance at Protestant church services never comes to more than 100 people all told, but there is a very high rate of turnover in membership, largely because of the strict rules of the sects: no drinking or entertainment of any kind is allowed, with the exception of singing hymns set to traditional Mexican folk tunes. There are services three to five nights a week, and members are expected to proselytize actively. The amount of time and energy required of Protestants causes many of them to leave the sects after a short time. Nevertheless, these ex-Protestants do not return to the Catholic Church but become secular, thus contributing to the general trend toward secularization in the village.

The Protestants of Buaysiacobe, unlike those in other parts of Mexico (Friedlander 1975:122), maintain established *compadrazgo* ties. Because many people join as adults, they have already acquired *compadres*. This continuity of a relationship deriving from the Catholic Church but important in everyday interaction means that there is less to give up by becoming Protestant. Protestants are not despised by their Catholic neighbors. They are ridiculed behind their backs, but there is always a crowd of onlookers at the doors of the churches when the hymns are being sung. The fact that being Mayo in Buaysiacobe is not inevitably associated with participation in the Mayo ceremonial system makes it possible to become Protestant and remain Mayo.

The appeal of the sects in Buaysiacobe is that of many social movements: usually conversion follows a personal or family crisis during which some sect members convince the individual of the efficacy of their prayers. After conversion, the conditions of social predictability and commitment discussed by Erasmus (1977:135-179) come into play. The congregations are small, and many members are related. The members call each other *hermanos* (brothers). Those who stray from the straight and narrow path are denounced before the congregation. Protestants also have a sense of prestige, because they believe they are the chosen people who will inherit the earth. Frequent meetings add to the sense of commitment to the group.

Compliance with the rigid rules against drinking and entertainment does not entail a rejection of all that the modern world has to offer. The sects are not ideologically opposed to wealth, and indeed pastors encourage their congregations to work hard, educate their children, and in general improve their material condition within the rules of the sect. One pastor informed me that he considered his spacious home and his truck a reward from God for right living. There is a certain amount of demonstration effect in Buaysiacobe of the rewards for being Protestant: the largest houses belong to Protestants or ex-Protestants, and four of the six ejido leaders are Protestants, ex-Protestants, or secular members of Protestant families.

The many similarities between the Protestant sects and the lower Mayo valley millenarian movement are perhaps less important than the fundamental difference: the latter movement rejects all of the Mestizo world, but the Protestants accept certain progressive elements. The Protestants are, in Aberle's framework, members of a redemptive movement. This type of movement aims at changing the individual members rather than the entire system. Aberle (1966:330) notes that "[t]hose redemptive movements with a focus on living in the world, rather than withdrawing from it, appeal to groups which are being pressed to occupy a new niche." The opportunities available to Buaysiacobe residents thus explain at least in part the relatively large number of fundamentalists.

Buaysiacobe is special in that Protestantism is fairly popular among the people of Mayo ancestry there. In Júpare, by contrast, there is a Jehovah's Witness congregation, but only one family from the Mayo side of the cultural continuum belongs. In Masiaca village there is also a Protestant church; its congregation is made up entirely of monolingual Spanish-speakers. The greater number of Mayo Protestants in Buaysiacobe can be attributed to the lack of concern over ethnic identity within the village. The ethnic and economic homogeneity of the community make for few occasions for any ethnic opposition. Economic mobility is possible for almost all the residents, and is therefore not linked with ethnic change. This lack of ethnic cleavage leads to a more casual attitude toward the connection between participating in Mayo folk-Catholic ceremonies and continuing to be Mayo. In a context where, in Aberle's terms, there are new economic niches to fill, fundamentalist Protestantism will be likely to flourish. On the other hand, the relatively sparse ceremonialism of the Buaysiacobe fiesta means that there is less to attract Mayos to participate than in Júpare or, for that matter, Masiaca.

Ethnic Continuity and Economic Mobility

Although there is a cultural continuum in Buaysiacobe (see Table 3), the economic status of the majority of the households in my survey is higher than that of almost any in the Júpare survey, including those at the Mestizo extreme (see Table 2). Despite this comparative wealth, 79% of the Buaysiacobe household heads claimed Mayo identity and half had two or more Mayo traits. Clearly, access to wealth in Buaysiacobe does not have the same ethnic implications as it does in Júpare.

TABLE 3. Ethnic Traits of Heads of Households and Income by Household in Buaysiacobe

Ethnic Continuum

	Mestizo				Mayo
	0	1	2	3	4
Low income	1	2	5	1	0
Middle income	0	1	3	0	0
High income	3	6	10	12	1

n=44

Note: The criteria for ethnic traits and economic status are the same as in Table 2.

Because being Mayo is not so closely tied to being poor as it is in Júpare, economic mobility is possible without ethnic change in Buaysiacobe. Those not considered Mayo are actually people who are not originally from the area. Some of the material and behavioral symbols used in Júpare to demonstrate ethnic change may be found in Buaysiacobe, but they do not mean the same things. Buying a television set or building a new house do not indicate a desire to be Mestizo. Participation in the religious aspect of the fiesta is so minimal that there are few opportunities to refuse to participate. There are no situations like Júpare's Wednesday Mass or Guadalupe velaciones to announce ethnic change.

In terms of the cultural continuum, however, there is certainly a lot of change going on in the village. The process of secularization itself is a major change in behavior and attitudes, and is evidently recent. Wealth, derived directly from the relatively large amount of land possessed by the ejido, makes possible a lifestyle unattainable by most Jupareños, including many of those on the Mestizo side of the continuum. The Buaysiacobe ejidatarios, like all rural people in the region, complain of their poverty, but they admit that Jupareños are indeed much poorer.

Buaysiacobe expresses the ideal of both development planners and some of the more recent writers on ethnic identity. This ideal is that, given adequate economic and social opportunities, ethnic minorities will be able to move into the larger society in economic and political terms, while still maintaining a separate ethnic identity--Furnivall's (1948) medley in a context of economic development. Buaysiacobe residents are not self-consciously ethnic in the manner of some members of ethnic minorities in the United States. Nevertheless, they do continue to call themselves Mayo and to speak Mayo. They also have many material possessions the ownership of which, in Júpare and many other villages, would define them as Mestizos.

This continuity of Mayo identity in the face of economic progress may, however, simply be a consequence of the relative rapidity of that progress. The fact that children are not learning Mayo and that parents are not making major vows for their children point to the possibility that future generations in Buaysiacobe will identify themselves as de razón. It may be that a change in that direction has already begun: although 37 of the 45 household heads surveyed claimed to speak Mayo, only 32 identified themselves as Mayos.

Because everyone is relatively wealthy, and because there is no historic basis for ethnic conflict, wealth does not indicate ethnicity by definition, as it does in Júpare. While most Buaysiacobe residents claim Mayo identity and are known to express ethnic pride at public gatherings, ethnicity is not generally a basis for action within the community. There is no pressure from family and kin to participate fully in the Mayo religious system, thereby sustaining Mayo culture. There is no automatic equating of Protestantism or outright secularism with Mestizo identity. Likewise, there are no ethnically defined situations that might contribute to ethnic cleavage and a consequent emphasis on maintaining Mayo ethnic identity. Given this fairly passive attitude toward ethnicity, and the relative wealth of the ejido, it seems likely that its current ethnicity will change in the next generation. The nature of that change will in all likelihood also be passive, unmarked by any recognized ritual dramas such as the Guadalupe velaciones in Júpare.

Situational Ethnicity

The expression of ethnic pride by Buaysiacobe residents is almost completely confined to the village and surrounding hamlets. In the city of Navojoa, the nearest market town, everyone is as Mestizo as possible. The restaurant section of the market is shaded by a large tree, and in this pleasant spot many regional-level political transactions take place. Ejido leaders from Buaysiacobe and other ejidos meet here informally with regional officials and bank agents in order to discuss ejido matters. No one speaks Mayo, and all dress in their best--cowboy boots, guayabera shirts, and Western-style straw hats are de rigueur. These people may speak of their fellow *campesinos*, but their conversations tend to be more symbolic than substantive. When the deals are struck, it is those most familiar with political matters and manners who come out ahead. These matters are for the most part better understood by people with more experience with Mestizo political affairs, i.e., people who are at the Mestizo end of the cultural continuum. Given this context, Buaysiacobe's leaders emphasize their political knowledge rather than their Mayo ancestry.

Women from Buaysiacobe go every so often to Navojoa to shop for fruits and vegetables that are not generally available in the village and very expensive when they are. Like the men, women do their best to appear Mestizo in the market or the shops. It is generally thought by Mayos and Mestizos alike that Mestizo shopkeepers find the Indians easy marks and will cheat them if they can. Of course, not all Buaysiacobe women are equally capable of behaving like Mestizos. It is not uncommon for a woman to go to Navojoa or even Ciudad Obregón to buy fabric and other goods, and then return to the village to sell some of her purchases to less enterprising housewives. These penny capitalists are toward the Mestizo side of the cultural continuum, although they generally declare themselves Mayo.

Situational ethnicity, then, is found primarily outside the community. This points to the possibility of full assimilation for the villagers in the future. The fact that they do not carry their allegiance to Mayo identity beyond the village is an indication that they are not proud enough of it to flaunt it to their detriment. It also supports the thesis that people behave in ways dictated by circumstances, based on prior experience.

Conclusion

Buaysiacobe is a special case in many ways. It is a community with enough of an economic base to make social mobility possible. It has used this economic opportunity well, and has prospered. At the same time, it has remained Indian, both as defined by the villagers and by Mestizo outsiders. It is small wonder that many government officials regard it as a showplace: it embodies many of the goals and ideals of the 1910 Revolution. It is productive, efficient, prosperous, yet composed of Indian peasants, the heroes of the Revolution. Its special qualities make it interesting, for it proves some of the basic tenets of both development and ethnicity theories. It has developed in response to adequate opportunities and has acculturated to the extent possible, given those opportunities, yet it has not lost its original identity. It has the best of both worlds. Whether or not this situation is permanent remains to be seen, however. The children in the community are not learning Mayo and are not being encouraged to be major participants in the folk-religious system. For them to grow up considering themselves Mayo without any observable Mayo traits would be remarkable, especially given the pattern of ethnic change in the region as a whole.

Even assuming that it is possible to retain ethnic identity with no ethnic traits, it is perhaps relevant to ask at this point the extent to which this success story can be repeated in contemporary Mexico. There is only so much land, only so much water, and these resources are now in the hands of entrenched private farmers in Sonora. If each family in Júpare could be given 20 hectares of irrigated land, it would probably develop along lines similar to Buaysiacobe, although some residue of ethnic cleavage would no doubt persist. Short of major social and economic changes, as well as technological breakthroughs, this kind of development cannot be hoped for in Mexico in the near future.

7

The Masiaca Comunidad

q: How do you earn your living?

a: From farming. I have nine hectares fenced but only three are cleared. Those I have planted right now to sesame, but it was no good because there was no rain.

q: And why haven't you cleared the rest?

a: Because I have no money, no strength, because we are poor. Right now we are with the bank; maybe they will help us to clear a little.

q: Do you have animals?

a: Three head of cattle. One has a calf, but I don't sell the milk because there is no pasture and there is only enough milk for the calf.

q: Why don't you plant vegetables in your yard?

a: We don't have running water, we have to bring water from the well.

q: Do you have a horse?

a: No.

q: Goats?

a: Six. A boy takes care of them, and when I sell one I give him part of the money.

q: How many goats do you sell in a year?

a: One or two. Sometimes I eat one. But when my wife was sick I sold eight good goats because I needed the money to buy medicine and pay the doctor. She was six months in the hospital in Huatabampo, and I had to pay for that. I sold four cows; I used to have eight. I was going to sell the rest, but my wife said, "don't sell any more, it's too much. I'm going to die anyway, and then you'll be left with nothing."

(interview with a member of the Masiaca comunidad, a widower, resident of an outlying hamlet)

Introduction

About 35 kilometers southeast of Huatabampo the Mayo Irrigation District ends and the vegetation reverts to the aboriginal thorn forest, which continues as far south as the Fuerte River Irrigation District in Sinaloa. The comunidad indígena of Masiaca, covering 300 kilometers (Erasmus 1978:48), is located in this arid region. The Masiaca creek runs through the comunidad and provides a limited amount of water for irrigation. The major source of income from the comunidad lands is livestock, mostly goats. The sparseness of the resources here makes for a sparse settlement pattern as well: aside from the village of Masiaca, the major pattern is one of small hamlets of from 10 to 150 households (CNEP census). These hamlets generally consist of one to ten extended families; the houses of those related through the male line are usually clustered together, for virilocal residence is the rule.

Life in these hamlets is probably very similar to that led by all Mayos before the coming of development. The living standard is well below that of the irrigated areas. Most hamlets lack running water, and those that have it usually have one tap for several households. The village of Masiaca has primary and secondary schools, but most *comuneros* live too far away to send their children to the village. All, on the other hand, have access to at least a four-grade school. Income is mainly from day labor in the irrigated region. There is a single bus that makes two trips daily from the city of Navojoa to Masiaca village; other than this, there are only a few cars and trucks that pass through the comunidad. Travel on foot or horseback is still the rule.

If it is sparsely settled today, even this density of population is made possible only by the development of the Mayo valley. The comuneros could not have remained here if they could not go to the large farms to the north periodically in order to work. Indeed, many young comuneros even today leave for years at a time to work elsewhere, usually sending money home or saving it to set up housekeeping in the comunidad upon their return. If there were not relatively stable work opportunities nearby, it is doubtful that many young men would return at all. Thus, development has made possible the continuation of a traditional, if poverty-stricken, way of life in the comunidad.

The Masiaca Comunidad

The church is the largest building in Masiaca village. However, it is rarely used by village residents, who are predominantly at the Mestizo end of the cultural continuum and consider themselves de razón. The comuneros see the church as belonging to the entire comunidad, not merely the village. They celebrate traditional Mayo folk-Catholic fiestas that are quite similar to Júpare's, although not quite so elaborate or frequent: Masiaca has two fiestas as well as the Lenten contis, while Júpare has four. There is a church at Las Bocas and a chapel in the hamlet of San José, but these do not have Mayo fiestas. The Las Bocas church was built by wealthy Mestizos who own beach houses in the community. The San José chapel has no fiesteros.

Role of the Instituto Nacional Indigenista

The INI has been active in trying to make the comunidad more self-sufficient. The agency helped Masiaca and two other comunidades indígenas to form a union in order to get loans from the Rural Bank. This union has been more or less successful in setting up a fishing cooperative, which provides jobs for 70 sons of comuneros. In many ways, the work pattern of the fishermen is similar to that of jornaleros: they are gone for several days at a time and at home for several consecutive days. The difference is that they are working within the comunidad, and they are more in control of the work situation.

Mayo control of comunidad affairs is in general a concern of the INI. Formerly, the Mestizos resident in the comunidad controlled the government not only of the village of Masiaca, itself mostly Mestizo, but of the whole comunidad. These leaders drew up a census that named all of the older comuneros but did not include their married children. The Mestizos' census also allowed people who had land outside the comunidad to be included as comuneros. After the INI set up its office in Etchojoa, it encouraged the comuneros to hold an election, in which Mayo leaders were elected to the comunidad government. They then drew up a second census, which included all married children of comuneros and excluded people with land elsewhere. The latter were for the most part Mestizo residents of Masiaca village. The second census features, of course, a great many more comuneros than the first: 2500 as opposed to 961. This issue may appear unimportant given the worth of the land, but there is always a hope that the Plan Hidráulico del Noroeste (PLHINO) will bring irrigation water to the comunidad. If this ever occurs, the land rights established by the current census will be extremely important. This success is directly attributable to INI intervention.

The INI has also set up a boarding school in Masiaca village for Mayo-speaking children. The school demonstrates the INI's basic goal of hispanicization of the Indians, for it features classes in Spanish. The school has only 50 beds, and thus can accommodate only a small number of eligible children. Because it, like the fishing cooperative, is quite recent, its impact on comunidad life cannot yet be assessed. It does at least contribute to a general sense of the worth of being Mayo comuneros.

Three Hamlets

The communities of San Pedrito, Jopopaco, and Las Bocas encompass the characteristics of comunidad hamlets, and also demonstrate the ways in which hamlets differ within the comunidad.

San Pedrito

San Pedrito is located just off the gravel road leading to Masiaca village, about 1.5 kilometers from the village itself. San Pedrito is a typical comunidad hamlet of 16 households, 12 of which are related by descent or marriage. San Pedrito has no school; the children walk to the four-grade school in Cucajaquia, 500 meters away. There are three water spigots in the hamlet, which has no electricity. All of the houses are adobe.

The president of the Masiaca church, who lives in San Pedrito and derives a small income from that office, is the only man in the hamlet who does not go regularly to the irrigated area to work, or to Las Bocas to fish with the INI cooperative. The male members of his family, the largest family in the hamlet, also earn money by occasionally performing as musicians at religious ceremonies, but none of them performs at secular dances.

Each household is headed by a comunero or the son of a comunero; if the new census is accepted, the latter would automatically become comuneros. Twelve of the households run small herds of livestock on comunidad lands; San Pedrito averages one cow or horse per household, and for medium livestock (goats and pigs) the average is 2.8 per household.

The one exception to the general pattern of poverty in San Pedrito is a man who is married to a woman of the predominant extended family. He owns two trucks, which he hires out for transporting workers to the irrigated area, or grain from the fields to the storage warehouses. This man speaks Mayo at home, but he is quite fluent in Spanish, unlike his wife and brothers-in-law. The latter call him a yori behind his back, and their reason for this is that he is wealthy but does not participate in the ceremonial system even by helping his relatives with fiesta costs. He calls himself a Catholic, but his affines say contemptuously that he is of no religion. He is considered ill-mannered and a troublemaker within the hamlet, and his relative wealth is clearly a source of envy and discord among the members of his extended family.

A contrast to this man is a woman who is also an in-law to the main family in the hamlet. She does not speak Mayo and never has, and all agree that she is not Mayo. Her behavior in daily life is so indistinguishable from that of other residents of the hamlet that her Mestizo standing is generally ignored. She understands some Mayo, she participates marginally in the fiesta system herself, and she does not object to her husband's sometimes prolonged absences while he plays the violin for the pascolas. She also bakes bread in her traditional Mayo oven, and is known for her ability at folk-curing. Because she behaves like most Mayos, she is fully accepted as a member of the family. She herself sees her inability to speak Mayo as a handicap, like her inability to read or write, not as a demonstration that she is Mestizo and somehow superior to other people in the ranchería.

These two individuals illustrate the nature of ethnic cleavage in the Masiaca comunidad in general: as long as everyone is equally poor, and participates however marginally in the religious system, the issue of ethnicity does not arise. If any family becomes somehow wealthier and drops out of the ceremonial system, its members are considered yori or, as in Júpare, "wanting to be yori." The process of becoming yori in San Pedrito, however, is not as formalized as in Júpare.

As a rule, ethnic identity is not an issue in San Pedrito. When asked casually if there are any Mestizos in the ranchería, residents reply that the Mestizos all live in Masiaca village; everyone in San Pedrito is Mayo. This is, objectively, essentially the case. Each household, for example, has a house cross and celebrates the Mayo version of the Day of the Dead, a practice abandoned even by most Jupareños. Mayo is the preferred language, and many people speak only broken Spanish. Four of the 16 heads of households and 4 children had major vows in the Mayo religious system. There are also 4 ritual musicians in the hamlet, a further indicator of Mayo identity.

Life in San Pedrito is much like life in the majority of the Masiaca hamlets; they are all similarly impoverished and remote from the developed area to the north. They are also generally regarded as very Mayo, as behavior and other traits indicate. Jopopaco and Las Bocas provide interesting contrasts to this pattern, for they each have unusual economic advantages.

Jopopaco

Jopopaco is a ranchería of 101 households (CNEP census) located two kilometers from the international highway and about 500 meters from the Masiaca creek. The hamlet has a four-grade school. Each household has running water but no electricity. Of the 15 heads of households interviewed, 12 work as jornaleros at some time during the year. However, because of the proximity of the creek, more families can count on irrigating a few hectares of land, thus insuring at least partial success in planting. Jopopaco averages 9 hectares of cleared land per household, as compared with 1.8 and 3.6 for San Pedrito and Las Bocas, respectively.

Because Jopopaco residents can easily walk to the nearby highway and take the frequent bus to Navojoa, they can get menial jobs there that are not so readily available to residents of San Pedrito. Similarly, Jopopaco children can continue their education in the city. The greater job and educational opportunities, and the larger amount of arable land, make for generally more prosperous conditions in Jopopaco than in most of the Masiaca hamlets. Economic and social opportunities are neither as numerous nor as stable as in Buaysiacobe. On the other hand, the availability of pasture land allows comuneros to invest money earned as jornaleros in livestock. The average household in Jopopaco has 10.4 cattle or horses and 10.2 pigs or goats, well above the average for any of the other communities in the study. This relative prosperity is expressed by house construction in the ranchería: two-thirds of the households in the sample boasted at least one room of brick, and half had four or more.

The economic level in Jopopaco makes for a rather ambivalent expression of ethnic identity. Some informants claim that there are no more Mayos in Jopopaco, because everyone is trying to become yori. Others say that if one is a comunero one is always a Mayo, at least in Jopopaco. Still others state that the offspring of Mayos are Mayos, even if they have no Mayo traits except for surname.

In fact, there is little that is Mayo about Jopopaco. Few houses have house crosses even during Holy Week; none of the households in the sample had house crosses. Although half the heads of households had completed major vows (e.g., fiestero, fariseo), none of the children had any vows at all. There is one family whose very religious elderly head has been a fiestero twice, but he is regarded as exceptional and a little crazy, even by his own family. A few old people speak Mayo among themselves, but none of their offspring speak it; this includes adults as well as children under 15. Despite this lack of Mayo traits, 46% of the household heads surveyed claimed Mayo identity.

There is little question that Jopopaco residents are on the Mestizo side of the cultural continuum. The process of acculturation has been pervasive: there are few differences in income, and most residents agree that conditions in the ranchería are superior to those of other hamlets in the comunidad. The relatively equal economic and social opportunities available to people of the community make possible the acquisition of Mestizo status symbols. At the same time, there is little pressure to remain Mayo, for there are no rewards for Mayo behavior, at least within the hamlet itself.

The pattern of ethnic change in Jopopaco is the most pervasive one in the valley as a whole. Those who experience upward mobility express this in ethnic terms by dropping the symbols of Mayo identity and acquiring Mestizo symbols. In Júpare and San Pedrito, the fact that those who "want to be yoris" are in a minority makes for a certain amount of tension surrounding this process. The economic marginality of those on the Mayo side of the continuum and the general shortage of opportunities for advancement lead them simultaneously to envy and reproach those who find a way to improve.

The underlying ethnic cleavage in Júpare and in the Masiaca comunidad as a whole leads to a situation where, in a context of few opportunities, economic mobility is defined as ethnic change and is scorned by the less fortunate.

In contrast to the situations in most Masiaca hamlets, economic and ethnic homogeneity, combined with the existence of some economic opportunities for all the residents in Jopopaco, have made for a fairly smooth path to cultural change. The lack of an underlying ethnic cleavage makes this change not likely to be resisted as traitorous to Mayo culture; the economic equality of the village leads to a passive acceptance of economic change as ethnic change.

This definition of ethnicity does not extend to situations where Mayos and Mestizos clash over comunidad matters, however. In the comunidad as a whole, the majority of Jopopaco residents side with the Mayo comuneros and against those considered Mestizo invaders. Likewise, Jopopaco residents attend the Mayo religious rituals, although they are not generally major participants. It is in the comunidad-wide context of long-standing ethnic conflict that the merest shred of Mayo symbolic behavior is brought forward; here, ancestry still overshadows current economic and ethnic realities.

Las Bocas

Las Bocas lies somewhere between San Pedrito and Jopopaco in both economic advantages and ethnic expression. This ranchería of 87 households (CNEP census) is located on the Gulf of California, about 12 kilometers from the international highway. Las Bocas has electricity, although not in all households, and each household has a water tap. There is also a six-grade school. The community's remoteness from public transportation routes isolates it for most of the year, but during Holy Week its aspect changes radically: the hamlet is invaded by hordes of Mestizo tourists, for Holy Week is the traditional Mexican beach holiday. There are about 75 houses built by Mestizos from Navojoa on the beach at Las Bocas which are used exclusively during Holy Week. The Mestizos pay yearly fees to the comunidad for the use of the land. Aside from the people who own beach houses, a great many visitors camp on the beach or arrive in campers and stay the whole week.

Although tourism represents only a small economic opportunity for Las Bocas residents, it nevertheless yields more income than is to be found in most comunidad hamlets. Various ranchería entrepreneurs peddle cooked food, fresh water, and cold soft drinks to the tourists, and income from these enterprises is not insignificant: a child selling soft drinks all day can turn a profit equal to the daily wage of an unskilled adult jornalero. To be sure, the boom is short-lived; it is, however, a dependable yearly source of cash for many residents.

Another special advantage Las Bocas has is the sea. Before the INI fishing cooperative was organized, many comuneros from the hamlet worked for private boat-owners, who paid them either a daily wage or a percentage of the catch. Some fishermen continue to work for independent contractors, but the majority now are members of the cooperative. The very location of the cooperative's headquarters in Las Bocas is a source of income for the residents, as the fishermen regularly patronize local stores and open-air restaurants.

Like Jopopaco, Las Bocas is on the Masiaca creek. Although the average amount of cleared land per household, three hectares, is smaller than Jopopaco's, it is still almost three times that of San Pedrito. The household average of 3.9 cows or horses and 7.5 goats or pigs is similarly intermediate between Jopopaco and San Pedrito. House construction, an indicator of wealth, also illustrates Las Bocas' prosperity: although most houses are adobe, three households in the survey had at least two rooms of brick, and only one house was of wattle-and-daub.

In terms of change along the cultural continuum, Las Bocas is also intermediate between the other two hamlets. Although Spanish is frequently spoken, most people still speak Mayo occasionally and the majority understand it. Significantly, one-third of the households had children under 15 who spoke Mayo. Half the households had children and two-thirds had adults with at least one major vow. In 25% there were house crosses all year long, and another 25% put up crosses during Holy Week. These statistics suggest that while Las Bocas residents are abandoning some Mayo customs and traditions to a greater extent than those in San Pedrito, they have by no means changed to the extent that Jopopaco residents have. However, because of the relatively equal economic opportunities in the hamlet and the general lack of concern over ethnic identity, ethnic change is similar in Las Bocas and Jopopaco in that it is associated with economic mobility but is not frowned on, as in San Pedrito.

Jopopaco and Las Bocas are extremes of ethnic change in the Masiaca comunidad. Because of special economic and social opportunities available to residents of these communities, the nature of ethnic expression is different from that in San Pedrito and the majority of the comunidad rancherías. Jopopaco and Las Bocas might be compared to Buaysiacobe in that the equality of opportunities makes for changes in lifestyle associated with being Mestizo, but their original ethnic homogeneity means that this change is not symbolic of abandoning the Mayo group, as it is in Júpare. Júpare's ethnic cleavage is somewhat more like San Pedrito's in that Mestizo behavior is interpreted as just that, and is discouraged.

These comparisons only go so far, however, for the level of wealth in Jopopaco, the wealthiest hamlet, is minor compared to Buaysiacobe's. In addition, the remoteness of most of the hamlets from the modern cities with their palatial mansions means that most comuneros are not reminded almost daily of their marginal status, as Jupareños are. Finally, the comuneros have a certain amount of power in the comunidad, and this makes for a greater degree of ethnic pride, at least in situations that bring out the Mayo status of the entire comunidad.

The Masiaca Comunidad

Ethnic Cleavage and Situational Ethnicity

q: Can you explain to me the difference between yoris and yoremes?

a: It is the very yoremes who have created the difference; they named the gente de razón "yoris," we call ourselves "gente de razón" in Spanish. Perhaps the Spanish named them "indígenas." That indígena, that yoreme, the one who is darker than the gente de razón or Spanish people, speaks *el dialecto* (Mayo) It is here in the humble towns that we always distinguish the people of the race (*gente de la raza*). They are more humble, more slovenly (*dejado*), maybe because of lack of education or because no one taught them how to live well, though many have means. It is the instinct of the blood.

(interview with a political official, resident of Masiaca village)

q: Are all the leaders in Masiaca yori?

a: Yes, and it's wrong, because for example the INI has told us that there should not be any yoris on the committees. In the meeting of the comunidad the other day, one of the yoris accused the INI and the bank of causing all the divisions in the comunidad, and that's a lie. The division was made by the yoris because they wanted more than the Indians; they want to take land away from the Indians.

(interview with a comunidad official, resident of a hamlet)

The daily life of comunidad hamlets clearly does not involve a great deal of concern with ethnic identity. In most rancherías, everyone speaks Mayo and only single individuals are sometimes condemned as yoris. People in Las Bocas and Jopopaco do not emphasize ethnicity, because they are changing economically. However, there is ethnic conflict, which surfaces in the context of affairs of the whole comunidad. For example, comunidad meetings are situations where Mayo behavior is expected. The meetings are carried on in Spanish officially, but Mayo is quite often used when individuals are making declarations or in private discussions about the issues involved in the meeting. In general, this is a context for the expression of anti-Mestizo sentiments, and the issues are most often couched in terms of ethnic conflict. Whereas in Júpare ejido meetings the enemies are always "*los ricos*" (the rich), at Masiaca comunidad meetings they are "*jumee yorim*" (those Mestizos). The Mestizos are accused of running cattle illegally on comunidad lands and of giving them comunidad water to drink. However, the most burning question during 1977-1979 was the census.

The proponents of the first census never attended comunidad meetings, which were overseen by INI agents, because they claimed the meetings were prejudiced against them. Instead, they circulated petitions in favor of their census. The faction that held meetings therefore had a public forum for denouncing their opponents as yoris who were trying to steal the comunidad lands from their rightful owners, the Mayos. The issue of the census rarely came up outside the context of meetings, unless I brought it up. Then, however it was the cause of the most violent outbursts I ever saw outside of drunken brawls.

All of the discussions at the comunidad meetings were more symbolic than substantive, for none of them was ever resolved. The meetings themselves were somewhat symbolic, for many people who attended felt that the matters under discussion either were never going to be decided on or would be decided by people in the government bureaucracy--the INI and the Rural Bank--not by the comuneros. However, there was a general consensus among my informants that if many people attended the meetings and made impassioned speeches, they had more chance of being heard than if they ignored the problems. In terms of ethnicity, the meetings also provide a forum for explicitly Mayo behavior as well as for expression of an opposition between Mayos and Mestizos.

Another situation favoring Mayo behavior is at the fishing cooperative headquarters in Las Bocas. The cooperative members are from all over the comunidad, and not all fishermen fish every day; thus the situation differs from life in the hamlets, where every individual's life history is known. The fishermen also realize that the cooperative was formed in an attempt to help them because they are Indians. Any fisherman who cannot speak Mayo is in some danger of being branded a yori, even if in his own hamlet it is known that his parents speak Mayo and therefore he could be considered Mayo. Thus, speaking Mayo is rather important. Mayo fishing terms are often used instead of Spanish ones, and the person who insists on speaking Spanish is not only treated with contempt but is also at some disadvantage in the work scene.

The fishing itself is done three men to a boat, and in this situation, too, Mayo-speaking ability is important--the boat boss selects his crew on the basis of their fishing ability but also takes into account whether they will be compatible and able to understand each other well; effective bilingualism is therefore an advantage. While working at the beach where the boats are stored and the fish collected and counted, Mayo is the preferred language as the fishermen bring in their boats, unload their catch, mend their nets, or simply rest and chat in small groups.

Still another situation favoring Mayo behavior is the Masiaca church on Sundays and at the fiestas. Masiaca's Sunday service is much like Júpare's:

the fiesteros gather at the church, say prayers led by a maestro, perform a ceremony with the fiestero flag, and clean the church. After this, they eat together with the maestro. There are few people there besides the fiesteros and church officials; however, Mayo is spoken by all present, and individuals who do not understand the ceremonies are rebuked. The subjects of conversation during the meal are also mainly of Mayo interest; they generally revolve around arrangements for the fiesta or discussion of who will be fiesteros the following year.

Masiaca also has Lenten Friday contis and Holy Week celebrations similar to Júpare's. There are only 20 to 30 fariseos at Masiaca, and 12 to 14 tres marías, compared to over 200 fariseos and 50 to 60 tres marías in Júpare. There are two fiestas aside from the Lenten and Holy Week celebrations: the Fiesta de la Bandera (flag fiesta) on February 24 and 25, where the new fiestero flag is initiated; and the main fiesta of San Miguel (St. Michael) on September 27, 28, and 29. These fiestas follow the regular pattern of all Mayo fiestas, as described in Chapter Three. The San Miguel fiesta is the only religious event during which there are also a secular dance, amusement rides, and games.

The Sunday service and the fiestas serve to reinforce the ethnic cleavage between residents of the village and the rest of the comunidad. In 1978, none of the fiesteros lived in the village and only 2 of the 12 lived as close as 5 kilometers away; 7 lived 8 to 16 kilometers from Masiaca, and 3 lived over 16 kilometers away. This is in contrast to the Júpare fiesteros, the majority of whom lived in Júpare or within 3 kilometers of the village. The Masiaca church officials likewise live in outlying hamlets.

Because the residents of Masiaca village are Mestizo and do not participate in the fiesta system, they view the Sunday service and the religious aspects of the fiesta as an invasion by benighted savages. The Mayos, on the other hand, see their participation in these events as an expression of their rightful place in comunidad affairs. The ethnic cleavage symbolized by the Sunday service and the fiesta is demonstrated by the heavy condemnation of Mestizo behavior at the church and by the boycotting of all Mayo religious events by Masiaca village residents. They watch the contis and other processions from their doorways, but they do not participate.

The contis and Holy Week celebrations, as well as the San Miguel fiesta, attract people from all over the comunidad. In 1978, there were 200 to 400 people at the contis; at the height of the Holy Week ceremonies there were at least 1500 people in attendance. The religious aspect of the San Miguel fiesta is similarly popular.

If Masiaca residents disdain the Mayo religious celebrations, this attitude does not extend to the carnival rides and secular dances that go along with them. People from all along the cultural continuum throng to these entertainments; as in Júpare, fiesteros and other ritual participants also go on the rides if they can afford to do so. This tradition is not new: 70-year-old informants claimed that their favorite part of the fiesta when they were children was the games. As in Júpare, however, this part of the fiesta is considered Mestizo, and Mestizo behavior is elicited in these situations. The Mestizo priest from Navojoa is not involved at all in the Masiaca fiestas, thereby making these affairs separate from all things Mestizo. Thus, Mayos participate in both aspects of the fiesta, but Mestizos only attend the Mestizo elements. This behavior is commented on by Mayos and Mestizos alike, and reaffirms the ethnic cleavage in the comunidad.

Masiaca residents, like the Mestizos in Júpare, have their own religious ceremonies. The remoteness of the village makes it more difficult for the Navojoa priest to say Mass frequently, but he does come once a month. On Sundays, catechism classes for the children are conducted in Spanish by a lay sister. This sometimes overlaps with part of the Mayo ceremony; each group ignores the other as much as possible, but they are aware of each other's presence: the fiesteros resent the presence of Mestizos in "their" church, and the lay sister once accused me of paying more attention to the "superstitious Indians" and ignoring her attempts to teach people the "true" religion, although I made an effort to divide my time equally.

Although other public events in Masiaca village do not necessarily reinforce ethnic cleavage, they are conducted entirely in Spanish and attended by self-declared Mestizos. These events include the meetings of the Padres de Familia and the consejo de bienestar; the topics discussed by both these groups have to do with improving the village and promoting its image as a "civilized" community. I never witnessed any anti-Mayo statements or behavior at these meetings, but the Masiaca police chief told me that it is because of the consejo de bienestar that the village has all the conveniences of villages in the irrigated region; implicit in this statement is the idea that because the village has hard-working, progressive Mestizos rather than lazy Indians, it has the best facilities in the comunidad.

This attitude is prevalent in Masiaca village, and serves to maintain an ethnic boundary inside the comunidad not found in either Júpare or Buaysiacobe. Thus, although in the hamlets there is little concern with ethnic identity, this does not indicate a lack of ethnic conflict in the comunidad. On the contrary, there is perhaps more conflict with ethnic overtones here than in Júpare, for there is less to unite those from the extremes of the cultural continuum and more to divide them. The greater degree of conflict is symbolized by actions at the comunidad meetings and at the fiestas.

Economics and Ethnicity in the Masiaca Comunidad

Initially one might conclude that in an area like Masiaca, where there are so few opportunities for mobility, both economic and ethnic change would be minor. In fact, the opportunities vary even within this seemingly homogeneous marginal zone. The proximity of the comunidad to the irrigated area provides more job opportunities than might at first seem apparent. Having land near the Masiaca creek or living by the sea confer greater advantages than are enjoyed by people in the remote interior of the comunidad.

San Pedrito has no nearby economic opportunities, for almost any income beyond that from livestock must be earned in the irrigated region. The ranchería is 10 kilometers from the international highway, and the trip to the workplace is so long that most jornaleros leave home for several days at a time. The disruptive effect on families keeps the frequency of these trips down, and the income level in San Pedrito is consequently depressed. Because of this poverty, anyone who is wealthier than the norm encounters the kind of envy usually attributed to peasants (Foster 1965); in San Pedrito, this envy manifests as accusations of being yori.

Las Bocas and Jopopaco both have greater opportunities than San Pedrito. For this reason, Las Bocas and especially Jopopaco are relatively wealthy. Equal access to these opportunities, as in Buaysiacobe, allows the people of Jopopaco and Las Bocas to acquire the accoutrements of Mestizo identity without fear of being called yori.

The contrasts in ethnic expression, and the interpretation of ethnic symbols as between Buaysiacobe and these two hamlets, are testimony to the complexity of ethnicity in this region. Buaysiacobe residents for the most part claim Mayo identity, although they display few Mayo traits. Residents of Jopopaco and Las Bocas are ethnically fairly neutral in everyday circumstances, although especially in Jopopaco there is agreement that Mayo symbols have been dropped. In contexts beyond the community, ethnic expression changes, however. In the wider forum of situations that include the entire comunidad, people from Jopopaco and Las Bocas tend to express Mayo identity. They side against Masiaca villagers at comunero meetings, and they attend the Mayo religious ceremonies at the fiesta. By contrast, Buaysiacobe ejidatarios make every effort to appear Mestizo outside their community, where Mestizo behavior is elicited.

Although ethnic identity is seldom the basis of symbolic behavior in the hamlets, ethnic conflict manifests between the people who live there and Masiaca village residents. Because there is no organization that brings these two groups together on a day-to-day basis, the economic and political issues that arise are dealt with in ethnic terms. Likewise, the religious system is manipulated by both Mayos and Mestizos in ways that bring out ethnic distinctions rather than smoothing them over, as in Júpare.

The variety of ethnic and economic behavior even in this apparently homogeneous area demonstrates the danger of making sweeping assumptions about the relationship between these two variables. It is safe to say that ethnic behavior changes in response to economic opportunities, but this should not imply that this change is of one kind or in one direction. At the same time, it is important to point out that in certain circumstances economic and political issues are expressed in ethnic symbols; to ignore this is to make ethnic expression appear less vital to life in the Mayo country than it actually is.

Conclusion

Economic Development in the Mayo Valley

Perhaps the most valuable lesson to be learned from the Mayo case is that economic development has complex and various effects. This is certainly not a surprising conclusion; the long history of the rise of capitalism is in many respects the story of the development of economic diversity. This diversity is sometimes ignored in the search for regularities when evaluating the effects of development programs. Much of the literature on development is concerned with the creation of a "model" of development that can be used anywhere and will have predictable results. The desire for such a program is understandable, given the realities of development agencies and national government planning. The Mayo example, however, demonstrates that the dream of a successful plan with a predictable, successful outcome is somewhat naive.

The Mayos were in many ways the victims of Mexico's development plan. Having fought for centuries to keep their homeland and their political autonomy, they lost both after being instrumental in bringing to power the very people who effected their disenfranchisement. Although many people of Mayo ancestry live better today than did their parents or grandparents, the monumental irony of their situation is not lost on them. Still, few would give up the minor improvements of their lot to return to the old days.

Mayos as a group were marginalized more than Mestizos by the process of development. Not only did they lose their lands and their autonomy, but they have not benefited from the results of this loss to the same extent as the Mestizos, better equipped in the first place to deal with the Mexican government and its economic policies by virtue of being Spanish-speakers. In terms of the trickle-down theory, those who were closest to the source of the trickle are those who now live in mansions in Navojoa and Huatabampo. On the other hand, many of those at the Mestizo end of the cultural continuum in the outlying hamlets and villages of the valley are little or no better off than their Mayo-speaking neighbors. The fact that only Mestizos are wealthy is, however, a point seldom overlooked by the poor.

Although it is true that in general those at the Mayo extreme of the cultural spectrum are more depressed economically than those at the alternate end, this fact obscures the economic diversity of the descendants of Totoliguoqui. The Masiaca comunero living in San Pedrito has very little in common with the Buaysiacobe ejidatario; their daily problems are vastly different, as are their general economic and political positions in the region. This diversity has come about for the most part since 1954; it is the result of the various opportunities created by development, as well as of historical and ecological circumstances. There were certain possible ways to develop the lower Mayo valley; the implementation of one of these plans led to the economic marginalization of much of the indigenous population. This marginalization is demonstrated by the case of Júpare. The region to the north and west had a different set of historical and economic circumstances, resulting in relatively greater opportunities to grow economically. The less dense population that made possible the distribution of larger plots in the area also made it possible for the Mayos of Buaysiacobe to progress economically more than many Mestizos in Júpare. The ecologically marginal area outside the irrigation district is in general also the most marginal economically, yet even here there is a diversity of economic conditions and ethnic expressions that are responses to historical and ecological circumstances as well as to economic opportunities.

Ethnic Identity in the Mayo Valley

If the San Pedrito comunero would be unable to understand the issues discussed at a Buaysiacobe ejido meeting, he would most certainly understand the pascola jokes at Buaysiacobe's fiesta. The Mayo language and the Mayo version of folk-Catholicism are virtually all that define Mayo identity; they are also what distinguish Mayo from Mestizo behavior within a given community. The extent to which an individual knows and speaks Mayo, and participates in the religious system, essentially defines his ethnic identity. Because these traits vary from individual to individual, the reality of ethnic identity in the Mayo area is actually a cultural continuum rather than two separate ethnic groups. It is meaningless to speak of ethnic boundaries, unless they be permeable membranes. The process of osmosis across these membranes is, however, one-way: people on the Mestizo side do not acquire the symbols of Mayo identity, but Mayo-speakers often consciously try to be recognized as Mestizos, in some cases on a permanent basis.

The extent of permanent cultural change and the degree to which it is couched in ethnic terms vary from community to community. Júpare's history of ethnic conflict as well as the presence of a sizable number of people from the Mestizo extreme of the cultural continuum create a context

Conclusion

for ethnic cleavage. The economic and political marginality of Júpare's Mayo-speaking population, in conjunction with the village's proximity to the enormous Mestizo wealth of Huatabampo, provides fuel for the continuation of this cleavage. Furthermore, any economic change tends to be defined as ethnic: to become wealthy is to become Mestizo. The existence of well-defined methods of changing ethnic identity, and of being recognized as Mestizo, shows how institutionalized this process is.

Buaysiacobe's ethnic and economic homogeneity makes for less emphasis on ethnic identity within the community. Because power and relative wealth are in the hands of people of Mayo ancestry, they are changing rapidly in response to the opportunity for modernization. This process, however, is not seen as ethnic change. Buaysiacobe's residents see themselves as Mayo, although they have few Mayo traits. This unusual situation may be short-lived, however; given the general pattern of ethnic change, it is likely that the children of Buaysiacobe will grow up to consider themselves gente de razón.

The lack of concern over ethnicity is seen to some extent in Masiaca's Jopopaco: ethnic homogeneity and equal economic opportunities make for social change that is not considered ethnic to the extent that it is in Júpare. In San Pedrito, however, ethnic identity is linked with economic status and participation in the religious system, as in Júpare. This difference in attitudes is attributable to the difference in economic and social opportunities. The situation of Las Bocas, intermediate between the other two hamlets, further substantiates the link between economic variables and the nature of change along the cultural continuum.

It is possible to locate an individual at some place along this contiuum by virtue of such criteria as language behavior and participation in the folk-religious system. Because of the complexity of behavior, however, many individuals can manipulate cultural symbols in order to comply with the behavior elicited by different situations. Situations, in turn, are defined in ethnic terms to the extent that ethnicity is an important issue in the community. In Júpare, because of the ethnic cleavage underlying much of the village's life, and because those at the Mayo end of the cultural spectrum have few economic opportunities, many situations are defined ethnically. Buaysiacobe's ethnic homogeneity, as well as its economic status, provide few contexts for ethnic cleavage. There is, likewise, little tendency to define situations ethnically. Masiaca's hamlets are relatively homogeneous economically, although economic conditions vary from hamlet to hamlet. There are few specifically ethnic situations in these hamlets, but the ethnic conflict between Mayos and Mestizos in the comunidad as a whole is more bitter than any I observed in the irrigated area. The rigid definition of ethnic situations at the level of the comunidad both expresses and reinforces this ethnic cleavage.

This study demonstrates that economic development causes cultural change. That point has, however, become something of a truism. The issue now is: What kind of economic development causes what kind of ethnic change? This question has a rather complex answer. In the case of the Mayo valley, there are economic differences as well as differences in historical and ecological circumstances in each community. There is also a wide variety of social and ethnic responses to this diversity, as illustrated here by only five of many hundreds of small communities in the Mayo region.

Without ignoring the extent of this diversity, it is possible to point out certain patterns of ethnic response to different economic and historical factors. Generally speaking, economic mobility is associated with the dropping of Mayo ethnic symbols. In communities where economic opportunities are unequally distributed along the cultural continuum, economic mobility tends to be defined clearly as a change in ethnic identity; this change is perceived negatively by those at the Mayo extreme of the cultural continuum. In these communities, ethnic identity and ethnic situations are given a great deal of importance, for they are expressions of economic and social status. It is in these communities that the ability to manipulate ethnic symbols is most useful, for social situations tend to be defined ethnically. The existence of an ethnic cleavage because of historical circumstances, as in Júpare, adds to the emphasis placed on ethnicity.

On the other hand, in communities where there are substantial economic opportunities that are distributed equally along the cultural continuum, economic status is not so tightly bound up with ethnic identity. People may identify as Mayo although they have few Mayo traits; this is the case in Buaysiacobe. Another response to economic equality, as in Jopopaco, is to be rather ambivalent about ethnicity. Here, residents do not consider ethnic identity important in daily life in the hamlet, but identify with their fellow Mayo comuneros in comunidad-wide ethnic situations. In any case, ethnic identity is not a burning issue within these communities, and ethnic conflict does not arise. This passive acceptance of culture change is even more common in communities where the population was originally homogeneous ethnically.

The Future of the Mayo Area

Economic progress has made for widespread changes in Mayo culture. The differences between the Mayo region in 1950 and 1980 are staggering, and they are for the most part the result of the Mexican government's development policies. These policies are tied to national and international events, however. Easy kinds of development such as the damming of the Mayo river have all been effected in Mexico; there are few possibilities for such dramatic development now, at least in Sonora. The Mexican government's dependence on the international oil market, and the consequences of that dependence in terms of the nation's international debt, have made for a situation in which even those minor development programs that might be possible in a more favorable economic climate are not likely to be implemented in the near future. The inflation that has plagued the country since 1977 has further eroded the possibility for economic progress in the country as a whole, and certainly in Sonora.

Will the end of dramatic growth mean the end of ethnic change in the Mayo region? This is difficult to predict. Ethnic change has continued even during the difficult years following the economic crises of 1976 and 1982; this suggests that it will continue to occur. The rate of that change, however, will probably be tied to the rate of economic change. Given this broad context, the fact that those on the Mayo extreme of the cultural continuum are economically and politically marginal with respect to the rest of the population in the region supports the notion that ethnic cleavages will not disappear in the near future. The 1913 Totoliguoqui uprising was based on economic and political grounds, but it manifested in ethnic terms. As long as ethnic identity is linked to economic and political status, there will no doubt continue to be Mayo Indians in southern Sonora.

Bibliography

Aberle, David F.
1962   "A Note on Relative Deprivation Theory as Applied to Millenarian and Other Cult Movements," in *Millennial Dreams in Action*, ed. Silvia Thrupp. *Comparative Studies in Society and History*, suppl. 2, pp. 209-214.

1966   *The Peyote Religion Among the Navajo*. Chicago: Aldine.

Acheson, James M.
1972   "Limited Good or Limited Goods?--Response to Economic Opportunity in a Tarascan Pueblo." *American Anthropologist* 74: 1152-1169.

Acosta, Roberto
1949   *Apuntes históricos Sonorenses: La conquista temporal y espiritual del Yaqui y del Mayo*. Mexico, D.F.: Imprenta Aldina.

Acuña, Rodolfo
1974   *Sonoran Strongman*. Tucson: University of Arizona Press.

Adelman, Irma, and Cynthia Taft Morris
1973   *Economic Growth and Social Equity in Developing Countries*. Stanford, Calif.: Stanford University Press.

Aguilar Camín, Hector
1977   *La frontera nómada: Sonora y la revolución Mexicana*. Mexico, D.F.: Siglo Veintiuno.

Bibliography

Alcantara, Cynthia Hewitt de
1976   *Modernizing Mexican Agriculture: Socioeconomic Implications of Technological Change, 1940-1970*. Geneva: UN Research Institute for Social Development.

Alegre, Francisco Javier
1841   *Historia de la provincia de la Compañía de Jesús en Nueva España*. 3 vols. Mexico, D.F.

Almada, Francisco R.
1971   *La Revolución en el estado de Sonora*. Mexico, D.F.: Talleres Gráficos de la Nación.

Almaguer, Tomás
1971   "Toward the Study of Chicano Colonialism." *Aztlan* 2 (1): 7-21.

Andrews, David H.
1963   "Paucartambo, Pasco, Peru: An Indigenous Community and a Change Program." Ph.D. dissertation in Anthropology, Cornell University, Ithaca, N Y.

Babchuk, Nicholas
1962   "The Role of the Researcher as Participant Observer and Participant-as-Observer in the Field Situation." *Human Organization* 21 (3, Fall): 225-228.

Bancroft, Hubert Howe
1884   *History of the North Mexican States and Texas*. San Francisco.

Banton, Michael, ed.
1966   *Anthropological Approaches to the Study of Religion*. New York: Praeger.

Barrera, Mario, Carlos Muñoz, and Charles Ornelas
1972   "The Barrio as an Internal Colony," in *People and Politics in Urban Society*, Urban Affairs Annual Reviews, vol. 6, ed. Harlan Hahn. Beverly Hills, Calif: Sage Publications.

Barth, Fredrik
1967   "The Study of Social Change." *American Anthropologist* 69: 661-669.

1969   *Ethnic Groups and Boundaries*. Boston: Little, Brown.

Bibliography

Beals, Ralph
1943 "The Aboriginal Culture of the Cahita Indians." *Ibero-Americana* 19.

1945 *The Contemporary Culture of the Cahita Indians.* Washington; D.C.: American Bureau of Ethnology.

Becker, Howard, and Blanche Geer
1957 "Participant Observation and Interviewing: A Comparison," *Human Organization* 16 (3, Fall): 28-32.

Beene, Delmar Leon
1972 "Sonora in the Age of Ramon Corral, 1875-1900." Ph.D. dissertation in History, University of Arizona, Tucson.

Benedict, Burton
1962 "Stratification in Plural Societies." *American Anthropologist* 64: 1235-1246.

Boissevain, Jeremy
1968 "The Place of Nongroups in the Social Sciences." *Man* 3 (4):542-556.

Bojórquez, Juan de Dios
1929 *Obregón: Apuntes biográficos.* Mexico, D.F.: Ediciones Nueva Patria.

Bram, J.
1965 "Change and Choice in Ethnic Identification." *Transactions of the New York Academy of Sciences*, ser. 2, vol. 28: 242-248.

Cancian, Frank
1965 *Economics and Prestige in a Maya Community.* Stanford, Calif.: Stanford University Press.

Castile, George P., and Gilbert Kushner, eds.
1981 *Persistent Peoples.* Tucson: University of Arizona Press.

Cohen, Abner
1974 *Two-Dimensional Man.* Berkeley and Los Angeles: University of California Press.

Comité Nacional para la Eradicación del Paludismo (CNEP)
1978 Raw Census data

Bibliography

Corral, Ramón
1900   *El General Ignacio Pesqueira: Reseña histórica del Estado de Sonora*. Hermosillo: Imprenta del Gobierno del Estado.

1959   *Obras históricas: Reseña histórica del Estado de Sonora, 1856-1877. Biografía de José María Leyva Cajeme. Las razas indígenas de Sonora*. Biblioteca Sonorense de Geografía e Historia.

Crumrine, Lynne S.
1969   "Ceremonial Exchange as a Mechanism in Tribal Integration Among the Mayos of Northwest Mexico." Anthropological Papers of the University of Arizona. 14.

Crumrine, Lynne S., and N. Ross Crumrine
1969   "Where Mayos Meet Mestizos: A Model for the Social Structure of Culture Contact." *Human Organization* 28 (1) 50-57.

Crumrine, N. Ross
1964   "The House Cross of the Mayo Indians of Sonora, Mexico: A Symbol in Ethnic Identity." Anthropological Papers of the University of Arizona. 8.

1968   "Anthropological Antimony: The Importance of an Empirical Basis for a Concept of Anthropological Fact." *Anthropological Quarterly* 41 (1): 34-46.

1975   "A New Mayo Indian Religious Movement in Northwest Mexico." *Journal of Latin American Lore* 1 (2): 127-145.

1977   *The Mayo Indians of Sonora: A People Who Refuse to Die*. Tucson: University of Arizona Press.

1981   "The Ritual of the Cultural Enclave Process: The Dramatization of Oppositions Among the Mayo Indians of Northwest Mexico," in *Persistent Peoples*, ed. George P. Castile and Gilbert Kushner. Tucson: University of Arizona Press.

Dabdoub, Claudio
1970   *Historia de el valle del Yaqui*. Mexico, D.F.: Librería de Manuel Porrúa, S.A.

Bibliography

Dow, James
1973 "Models of Middlemen: Issues Concerning the Economic Exploitation of Modern Peasants," *Human Organization* 32 (4, Winter): 397-406.

Dozier, Craig L.
1963 "Mexico's Transformed Northwest." *Geographical Review*, October: 551-568.

Dunbier, Roger
1968 *The Sonoran Desert*. Tucson: University of Arizona Press.

Erasmus, Charles
1952 "The Leader vs. Tradition." *American Anthropologist* 54: 168-178.

1961 *Man Takes Control*. Minneapolis: University of Minnesota Press.

1974 "Agrarian Reform vs. Land Reform: Three Latin American Countries," in *Contemporary Cultures and Societies of Latin America*, 2nd ed., ed. Dwight B. Heath. New York: Random House.

1977 *In Search of the Common Good*. New York: Free Press.

1978 "Culture Change in Northwest Mexico," in *Contemporary Change in Traditional Societies*. Champaign: Illini Books for the University of Illinois.

Foster, George
1965 "Peasant Society and the Image of Limited Good." *American Anthropologist* 67: 293-315.

Francis, E.K.
1976 *Interethnic Relations*. New York and Oxford: Elsevier.

Frank, Andre G.
1973 "The Development of Underdevelopment," in *The Political Economy of Development and Underdevelopment*, ed. Charles K. Welber, New York: Random House.

Friedlander, Judith
1975 *Being Indian in Hueyapan: A Study of Forced Identity in Contemporary Mexico*. New York: St. Martins Press.

Bibliography

Furnivall, J.S.
1948 *Colonial Policy and Practice.* London: Cambridge University Press.

Garibaldi, Lorenzo
1939 *Memoria de la gestión gubernamental del C. Gral. Román Yocupicio en el estado de Sonora.* Hermosillo: Imprenta Cruz Gálvez.

Geertz, Clifford
1963a "The Integrative Revolution," in *Old Societies and New States,* ed. Clifford Geertz. Glencoe, Ill.: Free Press.

1963b *Peddlers and Princes.* University of Chicago Press.

1966 "Religion as a Cultural System," in *Anthropological Approaches to the Study of Religion*, ed. Michael Banton. New York: Praeger.

1971 *Islam Observed: Religious Development in Morocco and Indonesia.* University of Chicago Press.

Germani, Gino
1980 *Marginality.* New Brunswick, N.J.: Transaction Books.

Gill, Mario
1960 *Episodios mexicanos: México en la hoguera.* Mexico, D.F.: Editorial Azteca.

González-Casanova, Pablo
1965 "Internal Colonialism and National Development." *Studies in Comparative International Development* 1 (4): 27-42.

1970 *Democracy in Mexico*, trans. Danielle Salti. New York: Oxford University Press.

Goodenough, Ward H.
1956 "Residence Rules." *Southwestern Journal of Anthropology* 12 (1, Spring): 22-37.

Gordon, Milton
1964 *Assimilation in American Life.* New York: Oxford University Press.

Bibliography

Hall, Linda
1981 *Alvaro Obregón: Power and Revolution in Mexico 1911-1920*. College station: Texas A&M University Press

Hansen, Roger D.
1971 *The Politics of Mexican Development*. Baltimore: Johns Hopkins Press.

Hardy, Robert William Hale
1829 *Travels in the Interior of Mexico*. London: H. Colburn and R. Bentley.

Hernández, Fortunato
1902 *Las razas indígenas de Sonora y la guerra del Yaqui*. Mexico, D.F.

Hicks, W.W.
1967 "Agricultural Development in Northern Mexico, 1940-1960." *Land Economics* 43 (4): 392-401.

Hu-Dehart, Evelyn
1981 *Missionaries, Miners, and Indians: Spanish Contact with the Yaqui Nation of Northwestern New Spain, 1533-1820*. Tucson: University of Arizona Press.

1984 *Yaqui Resistance and Survival: The Struggle for Land and Autonomy, 1821-1920*. Madison: University of Wisconsin Press.

Instituto Nacional Indigenista (INI)
1976 Raw census data, Mayo river region.

1977 Estudio socio-económico de la región de los Mayos. Etchojoa, Sonora (mimeo).

Keyes, Charles F.
1979 *Ethnic Adaptation and Identity*. Philadelphia: Institute for the Study of Human Issues.

1981 *Ethnic Change*. Seattle: University of Washington Press.

Lévi-Strauss, Claude
1963 *Structural Anthropology*, trans. Claire Jacobson and Brooke Grundfest Schoepf. New York: Basic Books.

Bibliography

Lewis, Oscar
1959 *Five Families: Mexican Case Studies in the Culture of Poverty.* New York: Basic Books.

Loehr, William
1977 "Economic Underdevelopment and Income Distribution: A Survey of the Literature," in *Economic Development, Poverty, and Income*, ed. William Loehr and John P. Powelson. Boulder, Colo.: Westview Press.

McClelland, David
1963 "Motivational Patterns in Southeast Asia, with Special Reference to the Chinese Case," in *Psychological Factors in Asian Economic Growth, pp.6-19, Journal of Social Issues* 19(1).

Medina, Francisco
1941 *Monografía de Sonora.* Mexico, D.F.: Talleres Modelo.

Mexico, Government
1853-57 Documentos para la historia de México. 20 vols. 4 series. Mexico, D. F.

Mexico, Government, Dirección General de Estadística,
1947 *Compendio estadístico.* Mexico, D.F.

1958 *Compendio estadístico.* Mexico, D.F.

1965 *Anuario estadístico de los Estados Unidos Mexicanos, 1962-63.* Mexico, D.F.: Talleres Gráficos de la Nación.

1970 Mexican National Census. Mexico, D.F.

1973 *Anuario estadístico de los Estados Unidos Mexicanos, 1970-71.* Mexico, D.F.: Talleres Gráficos de la Nacion.

Moore, Joan W.
1970 "Colonialism: The Case of the Mexican-Americans." *Social Problems.* Spring: 463-472.

Morawetz, David
1977 *Twenty-five Years of Economic Development, 1950-1975.* Baltimore: Johns Hopkins University Press.

Bibliography

Nagata, Judith
1974 "What is a Malay? Situational Selection of Ethnic Identity in a Plural Society." *American Ethnologist* 1 (2, May): 331-350.

1979 *Malaysian Mosaic: Perspectives from a Poly-Ethnic Society.* Vancouver: University of British Columbia Press.

Navarro García, Luis
1964 *Don José de Gálvez y la comandancia general de las provincias internas del norte de Nueva España.* Seville, Spain: Escuela de Estudios Hispano-Americanos.

Obregón, Alvaro
1970 *Ocho mil kilómetros en campaña.* Mexico, D.F.: Fondo de Cultura Economica.

O'Connor, Mary
1979 "Two kinds of Religious Movements Among the Mayo Indians of Sonora." *Journal for the Scientific Study of Religion* 18 (3):260-268.

1980 Ethnicity and Economic Development: The Mayos of Sonora, Mexico. Ph.D. Dissertation in Anthropology, University of California, Santa Barbara, Ca.

Pérez de Ribas, Andrés
1645 *Historia de los triunphos de Nuestra Santa Fee, en las misiones de la provincia de Nueva España.* Madrid.

Pinart, Alphonse Louis, ed.
n.d. *Documentos relativos a las misiones de la Nueva España*, 1781-1790.

Revilla Gigedo, Conde, Virrey
1794 "Ynforme general instruido en cumplimiento de la Real Orden de 31 de Enero de 1784 sobre las Misiones del Reyno de Nueva España." Letter. Mexico, D.F: Archivo General de la Nación: Correspondencia de los Virreyes.

Sahlins, Marshall
1981 *Historical Metaphors and Mythical Realities: Structure in the Early History of the Sandwich Islands Kingdom.* Ann Arbor: University of Michigan Press.

Bibliography

Sanderson, Steven E.
1981 *Agrarian Populism and the Mexican State*. Berkeley and Los Angeles: University of California Press.

Saravia, Atanasio G.
1937 *Ensayos históricos*. Mexico, D.F.: Imprenta Botas.

Saussure, Ferdinand de
1966 *Course in General Linguistics*, trans. Wade Baskin. New York: McGraw-Hill (1st French edition, 1915).

Shibutani, Tomatsu, and K.M. Kwan
1965 *Ethnic Stratification: A Comparative Approach*. New York: Macmillan.

Shils, Edward
1957 "Primordial, Personal, Sacred, and Civil Ties." *British Journal of Sociology*, June: 130-147.

Smith, Waldemar R.
1977 *The Fiesta System and Economic Change*. New York: Columbia University Press.

Sonora, Mexico, Government
1913 *Disposiciones relativas a la mensura y reparto de ejidos de los pueblos del Estado de Sonora*. Hermosillo: Imprenta del Gobierno del Estado.

1957 *Proyecto de programa de Gobierno del Estado de Sonora*. Hermosillo: Impresiones Modernas, S.A.

Sonora, Mexico, Province of
1764 "Materiales para la Historia de Sonora, 1658-1778." Manuscript.

Spicer, Edward
1970 "Contrasting Forms of Nativism Among the Mayos and Yaquis of Sonora," in *The Social Anthropology of Latin America*, ed. Walter Goldschmidt and Harry Hoijer. Berkeley and Los Angeles: University of California Press.

1971 "Persistent Cultural Systems." *Science* 174 (19, November): 795-800.

Stavenhagen, Rodolfo
1965 "Classes, Colonialism, and Acculturation." *Studies in Comparative International Development* 1 (6): 53-77.

Tovar Pinzón, Hermés, ed.
1971 *Lecturas de historia social y económica, Colombia y America: Fuentes para el estudio de las actividades socio-económicas de la Compañía de Jesús y otras misiones religiosas*. Bogotá: Universidad Nacional de Colombia.

Troncoso, Francisco
1905 *Las guerras con las tribus Yaqui y Mayo del Estado de Sonora, Mexico*. Hermosillo.

Turner, Victor
1964 "Betwixt and Between: The Liminal Periods of Rites of Passage," in *Proceedings of the 1964 Annual Spring Meeting of the American Ethnological Society*, pp.4-20.

1967 *The Forest of Symbols*. Ithaca, N.Y.: Cornell University Press.

1974 *Dramas, Fields, and Metaphors*. Ithaca, N.Y.: Cornell University Press.

Ulloa, Pedro N.
1900 *El Estado de Sonora y su situación económica al aproximarse el primer centenio de la independencia de la nación*. Hermosillo: Imprenta del Gobierno a cargo de A.B. Monteverde.

Wagner, Roy
1974 "Are There Social Groups in the New Guinea Highlands?" in *Frontiers in Anthropology*, ed. Murray J. Leaf. New York: Van Nostrand.

Wall Street Journal
1982 "Mexico's Peso Problems," Aug. 16, p. 1.

Wallerstein, Immanuel
1976 *The Modern World-System*. New York: Academic Press.

Walton, John
1966 "Discipline, Method, and Community Power: A Note on the Sociology of Knowledge." *American Sociological Review* 31 (October) 684-689.

Bibliography

Weber, Max
1970 *The Interpretation of Social Reality*, ed. J.E.T. Eldridge. London: Michael Joseph.

Wellhausen, Edwin J.
1976 "The Agriculture of Mexico." *Scientific American*, 235 (3, September): 128-153.

Wilkie, James
1970 *The Mexican Revolution: Federal Expenditure and Social Change Since 1910*. Berkeley and Los Angeles: University of California Press.

Williamson, Jeffrey
1965 "Regional Inequality and the Process of National Development,1 part 1." *Economic Development and Cultural Change* 13 (4, July): 203-219.

World Bank
1986 *World Development Report*. Oxford University Press.

Plates

Plate 1: Mayos unite in support of Obregón's forces (Obregón 1970:48).

Plate 2: Contemporary agricultural techniques in the Mayo valley.

Descendants of Totoliguoqui

Plate 3: The modern town of Huatabampo, Sonora.

Plate 4: One of the larger Mestizo homes in Huatabampo.

Plates

Plate 5: A typical home in the Masiaca comunidad.

Plate 6: A sesame field in the Buaysiacobe ejido.

Plate 7: The Júpare ramada, with the village flag indicating that there is a fiesta in progress.

Plates

Plate 8: Masiaca fariseos.

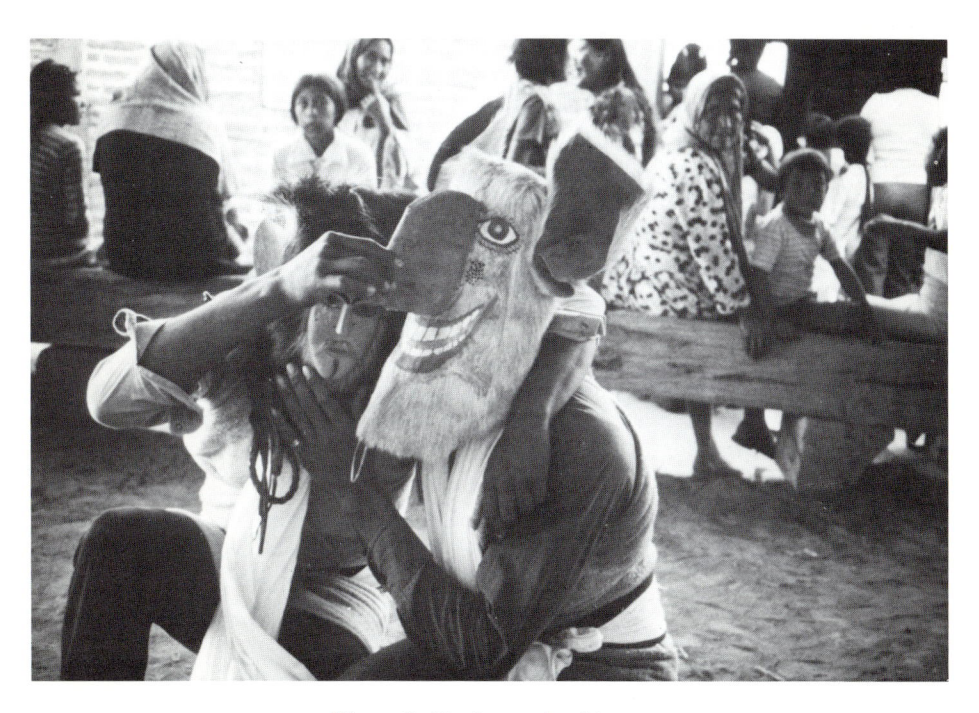

Plate 9: Fariseos in Júpare.